# DESIGNING PROGRAM ACTION— AGAINST URBAN POVERTY

# DESIGNING PROGRAM ACTION—
# AGAINST URBAN POVERTY

**George A.** Anderson **Shipman**

The University of Alabama Press

UNIVERSITY, ALABAMA

# Contents

### Charts

# DESIGNING PROGRAM ACTION— AGAINST URBAN POVERTY

# Introduction

THE SUBSTANCE OF THIS STUDY WAS GIVEN IN THE Southern Regional Training Program Annual Lectures, November 18–22, 1968, at the University of Alabama. As presented here, the materials have been reordered to some extent, and commentaries on source materials and ideas have been updated. The style and scope of the five lectures, however, have been retained. The aim was to convey an overview of an approach rather than to present a technical analysis in the depth that obviously would be possible.

The original effort from which the lectures developed was an aspect of the Social Change Evaluation Project undertaken at the University of Washington by a faculty group under contract with the Office of Economic Opportunity (OEO Contract 1375). This project undertook a comprehensive evaluation of the impact of the Community Action Program of the Seattle–King County Economic Opportunity Board upon the Seattle–King County community. The evaluation effort was designed around a series of research probes directed toward several areas of major impact. Each of these probes was separately designed and separately prosecuted. To bring them, and especially their inferences, together in a coherent and comprehensive evaluation of the program as a whole, an overall design was essential. One was developed by projecting an ideal analytical model of a comprehensive community action program, relying primarily upon a set of systems ideas and approaches. This model then became the framework for interrelating the findings of the various research probes and the point of departure for reaching conclusions about the general effects of the community action program.*

The problem of poverty offers a useful context for exploring the implications of comprehensive broad-aim, broad-impact programs aimed at socioeconomic change. The implications of poverty are multidimensional. It weighs upon government at every level, because competence to intervene is spread throughout the governmental system. But it weighs not upon government alone. Action capability is not limited to government although, in terms of funding and comprehensiveness, the major competence is there. There is the voluntary sector, in many urban areas an essential provider of social and rehabilitative services, and often the primary professional and technical resource for the design and administration of such activities. The potential contribution of voluntary efforts in innovation and experimentation is especially significant. There is the private sector, with an influence that is always strong, if often rather subtle. Employment practices, especially in employment and training of nonwhites, and informal requirements for labor union membership, are noteworthy variables. Cultural and subcultural values can interpose barriers to the socioeconomic mobility of minority racial groups, limiting the aspirations of their members

* See *Social Change Evaluation Project*, Final Report, Volume II, George A. Shipman, Principal Investigator, University of Washington, Seattle, Washington, 1968. The ideas underlying the experimental model are sketched in Ch. VI, "Working Papers," pp. 91–126.

to low status and relatively low income pursuits and to marginal, and often submarginal, residential areas. The relatively open society can still shelter essentially rigid patterns of socioeconomic stratification. Altogether, the whole of the society is involved with the condition of poverty.

The primary concentrations of contemporary poverty are in the urban centers. The contributing reasons are multiple; the fact remains. Rural poverty is a real and present problem, but functionally a somewhat different one. In any case, the urban area is the concern here. Poverty is a reality of the urban area, and one with which urban government must deal. Yet American cites, taken generally, lack the jurisdictional authority, the fiscal competence, the administrative resources, and the operating experience to deal with the causes and effects of poverty, however defined. They have the primary context in which poverty develops and persists, and they do not have means for dealing with its causes or its consequences.

This book is not a treatise upon the impotence of the cities or a prescription for their ills. Nor does it propose a confident solution for the poverty dilemma. The effort, both modest and experimental, is to estimate how certain emerging approaches to program design and evaluation can be applied to such problems as urban poverty.

For present purposes, the primary concern is not with the nature of urban poverty or with the intervention strategies required to deal with poverty in any specific context. The primary concern is how an intervention strategy can be designed by employing a set of systems ideas for modeling an action program that can utilize available resources in the public, voluntary, and private sectors. Ideas and assumptions about the nature of poverty, the causes of the condition, and the lines of action adapted to alleviate poverty become part of the approach, but this study is not aimed at weighing the theoretical validity or the operational effectiveness of these ideas. The purpose, much more limited, can be stated as a question. How could reasonable persons, not committed to any doctrinal approach to the alleviation of poverty, utilize a set of ideas to design and prosecute an intervention effort that would yield, through feedback data, indications of the extent to which the effort was realizing its objectives, and whether the objectives contributed to the alleviation of poverty in a specific urban context?

The underlying working assumption used here is that emerging applications of systems theory will permit the design and administration of problem-solving undertakings in the urban context, efforts in which the urban administrator, whatever his formal title, becomes the designer, the catalyst, and to an extent the manager of operating systems utilizing productive capacities that stem from a variety of jurisdictional and functional bases. Indeed, it is possible to visualize comprehensive intervention efforts in which the municipal government, in terms of its ongoing services and activities, has no more than minimal operating participation. This may be the shape of the more significant forms of urban administrative leadership in the years ahead.

Many persons contributed to the development of the approach presented in these lectures. The members of the Project Steering Committee of the Social Change Evaluation Project at the University of Washington, in discussions of the working papers, contributed insight, clarification, and criticism. They were Charles B. Brink, Dean, School of Social Work; Irving N. Berlin, M.D., Professor, Psychiatry and Pediatrics, and Head, Division of Child Psychiatry; Eugene C. Elliott, Associate Professor, Humanistic-Social Studies, and Special Assistant to the President of the University; J. B. Gillingham, Associate Professor, Economics; Edgar M. Horwood, Professor, Civil Engineering, and Director, Urban Data Center; T. Fred Lewin, Associate Dean, School of Social Work; S. Frank Miyamoto, Professor and Chairman, Sociology; Luvern V. Rieke, Professor, School of Law; and Jack A. N. Ellis, Assistant Professor of Social Work and Project Director. Among academic colleagues, Professor Fremont J. Lyden, Graduate School of Public Affairs and also associated with the Project, contributed notably to the development of the theoretical construct. Many students, candidates for the MPA and Ph.D. degrees, tested the central ideas in course discussions and projects. Mrs. Barbara Stickel translated illegible script into workable typed drafts. My wife, Evelyn N. Shipman, ever a staunch defender of the purity of language, edited the manuscript. All errors and eccentricities, however, remain my responsibility.*

Grateful acknowledgment is due Professors Robert Highsaw and Coleman B. Ransone, Jr., of the University of Alabama, whose gracious hospitality made my week at the University a most stimulating and rewarding experience.

GEORGE A. SHIPMAN

*University of Washington*
June 1970

---

* Certain ideas and concepts are expressed in these papers by means of terms that may be unfamiliar to some readers. The terms and their interrelationships are explained in the appendix.

# I

# The Problem of Urban Poverty

PERSISTENT SOCIAL AND ECONOMIC PROBLEMS plagued a prosperous United States in the 1960s. The private and voluntary efforts of the society and a variety of efforts by government were not availing to stem the decay of the cities, to meet needs for education, housing, and local economic development, to resolve or even to mitigate the problem of poverty. The conviction grew that such problems could be resolved or contained only by a new approach, a new strategy that would mobilize all resources of the society into mutually reenforcing cooperation. The goal expressed in the Federal program of the Great Society signified this conviction and was a response to it as well.

The approach recognized the national scope of basic problems. James Sundquist points out that, during the decade, Federal aid investment in state and local problem-solving more than tripled in total amount, and broadened to encompass an additional 39 fields of state and local activity. But the diversity of local action requirements was also recognized. A unique action strategy developed. The Federal government was to be entrepreneur, stimulator, reinforcer, and underwriter. But active planning and operation of the action programs were to be local and were to involve the private and voluntary as well as the governmental sectors. The symbolic label "community action" epitomized the approach. The War on Poverty, initiated in 1964, put community action to the test of producing a state of affairs in which the causes of poverty would be controlled and the consequences of poverty allayed. The objective, so stated, is less than precise, but it seems to be the substance of the statutory rhetoric that declared the War. The declaration did make clear that the major impact and the primary investment were to be made in the urban areas.

This inquiry into the implications of carrying out a policy and operating commitment of this nature and these proportions takes the War on Poverty as the working example. In setting the framework for consideration of the special problems and requirements of such a program effort, this chapter examines three interdependent sets of factors. The first is the nature of poverty. If the objective is to control the causes and consequences of poverty, the nature of the condition, the primary causative factors, and the points for effective intervention must be defined, at least operationally. Second, if the target, for purposes of this analysis, is the urban area, the action capabilities of urban areas must be considered. Admittedly, circumstances vary widely. Nonetheless, some summary or generalized overview is essential. The third factor is community action. What in this approach conditions the design and operation of intervention to cope with the condition of poverty?

*Poverty*

What is poverty? What are its attributes? What causes it? Value judgments and subjective preferences cluster around these questions, and proliferate in responses to them. But presumably there can be a working definition of the "poor" as distinct from the "non-poor." The difference may be only between points on a continuum of socioeconomic attributes. But the difference must be measured, and a relatively sharp breaking point set, if an intervention strategy is to be devised. It is also necessary to identify poverty's causes—the influences or forces without which the condition, as operationally defined, would not exist.

It is in order, then, to consider the difference between the observed state of "poverty" and an assumed state of "non-poverty." The gap measures the proportions of the problem; the nature of the difference identifies the characteristics of the problem. There seem to be at least six ways to regard poverty. These viewpoints, much oversimplified, follow in summary:

1. People are poor when they do not have access to the "social utilities" deemed essential to a reasonable quality of life. Environmental factors are prime concerns here. Submarginal housing, the lack of recreational facilities, inferior education, inadequate health services, and the like add up to an environment that tends to produce and to perpetuate poverty.

2. Poverty is the position of the lowest income groups in relation to the rest of the national society. This can be seen as a matter of economic inequality. Measures to increase the economic income of the lower levels would narrow the income gap and thus reduce the incidence of poverty. Emphasis would be upon subsidies, transfer payments, and, where applicable, cost-free services.

3. A third approach questions the first two and emphasizes social and economic mobility. The argument is that the poor, and particularly the non-white poor, lack the opportunity to alter their income, occupa-

tional, and social positions. Social stratification blocks their escape from the context of poverty, even when they have adequate income.

4. A fourth point of view emphasizes social maladjustment and the problems of alcoholism, delinquency, mental illness, illiteracy, illegitimacy, and the like. The poor are poor because they are the victims of the social ills afflicting them, and the presence of these ills tends to perpetuate a sort of social pathology. The consequences are low motivation, little initiative, and an indifferent attitude toward opportunities for self-improvement. Social and familial stability are assumed to underpin economic self-sufficiency in this view, and thus it often emphasizes behavior characteristics regarded as dysfunctional in the middle-class society. Intervention to alter these patterns, it follows, would reduce poverty.

5. The fifth approach puts adjustment and pathology to one side and emphasizes the behavior of the major institutions of the society. It is argued, often with special reference to education, employment, and law enforcement, that these institutions function in a way that excludes the participation and the special concerns of the poor, and leaves them isolated and powerless to express and to protect their special concerns. For the poor, there results a loss of dignity and self-respect, a drift into apathetic isolation.

6. The sixth point of view is concerned with the operation of the economic system. It is argued that a residual group of the low-skilled is continuously unemployed, or employed only at times of extraordinary demand for labor. Some of this unemployment is inevitable, even necessary to the operation of the economy. Economic

policies that stimulate full employment will reduce the size of the group. A related contention is that the provision of money income to this group feeds money into the income stream and thus becomes an economic stimulant. The way to deal with poverty is by influencing the operation of the economy, not by direct services or remedial treatment for the poor. The poor benefit as a byproduct of the management of the economic system; the strategy of this management is the primary determinant of the amount and nature of poverty.

What action will reduce poverty? Presumably the objective is change, a modification representing a reduced incidence of poverty. Depending upon the definition of poverty accepted as controlling, the change, and probably some mix of change, could be in the environment in which the poor live, in the distribution of income, in occupational opportunity and mobility, in the perceptions, aspirations, and behavior of people, in the distribution of power to influence the performance of institutions, and in the operation of the economic system.

These approaches to intervention can be grouped generally into four action strategies—the allocation of resources, the treatment of social maladjustment, the performance of critical institutions, and the operation of the economy. The last, the economy, seems to assume that an effective economic strategy will so involve the poor that the income gap will be narrowed to the point where serious dysfunctions no longer exist. Presumably, some degree of social pathology is involved in a lack of income, but action to eliminate this pathology need be only temporary and transitional. Of course, the utility of this strategy depends upon the validity of the assumptions that poverty is essentially an economic condition, and that the economy can be stimulated to a point of near full employment without inflationary consequences more serious than the amount of poverty relieved.

A strategy of resource allocation to remove insufficiencies in adequate housing, nutritional levels, health services and the like, with accompanying investment in skill training to prepare for employment, has considerable appeal. The difficulty is that available research fails to confirm any clear association between these conditions and poverty. There is no convincing evidence that the incidence of morbidity is higher among the poor than among the non-poor. The relationship of low income, because of low skills, to poverty seems to exist, but the interdependence of the two is elusive and complex. Environmental circumstances can be improved, and economic poverty relieved, by a reallocation of resources, but the problems of poverty may remain untouched to the extent that the primary causes are rooted in a lack of mobility, social pathology, and institutional performance. Nevertheless, if people who lack environmental amenities and minimum income are operationally defined as poor, an action strategy to change these conditions will reduce poverty so defined, even if this result is only a self-fulfilling prophecy.

Reduction in social maladjustment, or pathology, would reduce the incidence of poverty if there is a valid causal relationship between the two. But is there such a relationship? Do prejudice and social stratification contribute to poverty except by definition? What are the clear causal relationships? What about the argument that equalization of opportunity runs the risk of intensifying a sense of failure, and consequently the problems of personal adjustment? The connotation of a culture of poverty is apparent here. The basic assumption seems to be that a tangle of pathology prevents people from responding to opportunities. The life style of the poor has cultural deficiencies that set in motion a self-perpetuating cycle characterized by apathy and social disengagement. Rehabilitative strategies,

stimulation of self respect, of career motivation, of the utilization of available institutional services, will help to break the
cycle of poverty. The difficulty is that the existence of the cycle
and of the causal relations attributed to it are not demonstrated.

The action strategy of institutional performance rests upon
the working assumption that the critical institutions of the
society operate so as to reenforce and perpetuate poverty. The
critical institutions are those with the capacity either to contribute significantly to social and economic mobility, or to block
the efforts of the motivated poor to escape from the context of
poverty. Here again would seem to be the hypothesis of a self-
perpetuating culture of poverty, and also the idea that latent
motivations and capacities among the poor, if stimulated and re-
enforced, can develop into manifest and constructive drives.
The notion of widespread social pathology is implicit in the
idea of a dysfunctional culture of poverty and may not be
wholly consistent with the idea of latent motivation and capacity. Nonetheless, the emphasis is upon inducing change in the
functioning of the institutions of public education, social services, law and the courts, and governmental services generally,
so that fully adequate support is extended to the poor to escape
from poverty. The question may be raised whether the aim is
universally applicable services, according substantially equal
treatment to all, or differentiated services, extending special
treatment to those defined as poor. Equal services might in
effect favor those best equipped to respond, and thus tend to
bypass the "hard core" of the poor. Differentiated services
would amount to positive discrimination in support of the poor,
thus stigmatizing them as a special lower-class group. There
may be a further subtle assumption here, that the function of
these institutions is to push the poor toward acculturation to
dominant middle class norms and behavior patterns. The infer-
ence is that since the poor seem to lack or reject these norms

and patterns, such rejection is a dynamic element in maintaining the condition of poverty. This suggests that there is a causal relationship between the values and behaviors of the middle class society and "non-poverty." No clear empirical evidence for such a position seems to be available.

A critical question hangs unanswered over all of these approaches. How can the effectiveness of action be measured? The question becomes critical because of the speculative nature of the assumptions underlying alternative approaches. Where a battery of approaches is employed, the consequences of any one type of action can be blurred by the cross-cutting influences of others. Some types of action may be complementary and mutually reenforcing. Others may be sufficiently inconsistent that the impact of one is minimized by the presence of the other. To be sure, some operational definition of poverty could be adopted and the gross impact of a comprehensive, multi-faceted attack could be appraised. But the utility of any one component would be almost impossible to see except by the use of suboptimizing analysis.

Cost-benefit analysis is suggested, but at this stage of its development, the technique has very limited utility. Reliable data are lacking, questions of values and preferences are subtle variables, and cause-effect relationships are problematical. There is much to be done to bring this technique to operationality in the social services, especially with respect to such problems as poverty. Another approach to measuring effectiveness would rely upon the market place. What is responded to by the poor could be regarded as useful and effective. Where there is little or no response, emphasis would be reduced or the effort discontinued altogether. Again, the political process may be used as a kind of empirical test. What attracts political support will be pushed; what lacks support will be dropped. But underlying both the market place and political tests are subsumed values that, upon analysis, may prove unacceptable. Until much more solid and validated knowledge is available, the critical decisions of utility and effectiveness are ultimately open to influence by subtle or explicit value preferences, whether the decisions are made in the legislative, the administrative, or the research context. Even these choices can be blurred when decisions are reached by a pluralistic method of appraisal involving the intertwining of a variety of viewpoints and expectations. The way to judgment is not simple or easy.

## The Urban Context

The current literature treating the American urban scene is substantial in volume and diverse in content and emphasis. No summary or review of that literature is intended in the few broad interpretations of trends that follow here. Other aspects of the urban scene apart, these seem to have importance as influences conditioning the setting of urban poverty.

Population of the larger urban area, the conurbations, is growing. But the significant increase is in the outer ring, while the central city is either static, or is losing population.

Economic activity appears to be moving steadily toward predominantly white-collar employment in the inner city, with manufacturing showing an absolute decline in the central city and a steady increase in the suburban ring. Wholesaling and services, measured by employment, show practically no growth in the central city, but substantial expansion in suburban areas.

Available data show the poor tending to cluster in low-cost, depreciated housing in the inner city or in an inner ring. Their location is controlled by the availability of shelter rather than by preference. Substantial numbers of the poor and the near poor are aged. Those in the adult working years tend to be low-skilled or impaired; they are on the periphery of the labor force.

Many of the impacted poor are members of minority groups. The characteristics of the poor, however, appear to vary among urban areas. Indeed, each urban context has unique characteristics. Some combination of the same basic factors, those just sketched, can be assumed to be present, but there are differences in the mix, and in the relative influence of one set of factors over others.

The fiscal capacity of central cities is not keeping pace with rising service costs and the need for replacing obsolete urban plant. The property tax has obvious difficulties in administration, revenue yield, and equity. Other forms of taxation are difficult to use except over a fairly wide economic area, an area usually considerably larger than the city itself. The suburban ring has its own problems of expanding service needs and the cost of capital outlays. Financial supplementation from larger jurisdictions, the states and the Federal government, is gradually developing, but usually for special purposes or for major project reenforcement. Fiscal stability for the cities is far from realization.

The governmental competence of most cities is circumscribed. Even where "home-rule" is in effect, realistically the capacity to act is confined by general state legislation and narrow fiscal competence. The city is still a subordinate instrumentality of the state and the states are for the most part still dominated by non-urban concerns. The direct activities of the cities and a rough distribution of emphasis among them can be estimated from a sample of city budgets. The protection of persons and property, the provision of facilities for traffic movement, the development of recreational areas, and land use control are salient. The common utilities such as water supply, sanitation and sanitary sewers, and solid waste disposal are likely to be specially funded, self-supporting operations. With certain prominent exceptions, social services are usually not a city re-

sponsibility. Where they are administered through the municipal government, the nature of the activity is that of a delegated
state function rather than a fully local one. Public education
is administered in most states by a separate local jurisdiction,
usually with its own tax levying authority. Altogether, the
contemporary urban government is primarily equipped to
develop and maintain a physical environment, and to protect
its residents in the use of this environment. It can be argued that
urban government is used in the American culture to produce
a relatively benign environment—benign, that is, in terms of the
tastes and preferences of the dominant local groups—for the
realization of all reasonable aspirations of the residents of the
area. The realization is for the most part unstructured and
voluntary; organized activity is more likely to be nongov-
ernmental than governmental. Urban government, generally
speaking, is not geared to socio-economic problem solving. The
unspoken assumption is that such efforts are rooted elsewhere,
the city collaborating within its limited capability.

The evaluation, summary and impressionistic, is not intended to be harsh. There is little reason to conclude that the
American city, at least since the Great Depression, has been
expected to cope with problems of poverty and socio-economic
disadvantage. Clearly it has not developed any substantial capacity to do so. It seems fair to say that American urban government, confronted by urgent pressure to ameliorate impacted
poverty, finds itself without adequate authority, poorly fi-
nanced, without qualified staffing, and hopelessly inexperienced.

## Community Action

The idea of community action includes considerably more
than the capacity of the primary local jurisdiction, usually
the city. Initially the community is seen as the focus of poverty

occurring in some pattern of more or less interrelated locations. These locations may be concentrated in a single relatively compact area, occupying only part of an urban jurisdiction. Under other circumstances a number of impacted poverty locations, socially and economically linked by common influences, may be scattered seemingly at random over a central city and its satellites. A working idea of community is applicable in either instance, and in others, because of the linkages among the poverty clusters and the non-poor and more affluent social components of the area. The community in these terms is the immediate task environment. There is also the implicit idea of community resources and capabilities, including not only the local jurisdictions but also the operating capacities of the Federal and state agencies having an impact, actual or potential, upon the community. But more than the public sector contribute to community problem solving. Voluntary agencies are a significant resource in many locations, and the private sector is most likely to have the job training and skill development capability, while also supplying the primary employment market. Thus the idea of community as task environment can be seen as land area and population with patterns of social and economic linkages, and equipped with some degree of problem solving capacity among the public, voluntary and private sectors of its life. The mobilization of these capabilities, reinforced by Federal supports, to realize a significant impact upon poverty as it exists in that particular context, is of the essence of community action.

Wherever this idea of community action becomes an option for socioeconomic problem solving, basic questions arise. Is the method applicable to the problem? What is its utility? In the light of whatever may be known about the nature of the problem, what significant difference can this style of action be expected to accomplish? To illustrate an approach to estimating community action capability, in this case with respect to urban poverty, the four action strategies of intervention will be considered again in the context of the community's capacity to employ them. For the moment, all four strategies will be assumed to be potentially effective, and community capability will be treated as a generalized attribute of a middle sized metropolitan area.

The operation of the economy can be put aside as beyond the reach of community action. To be sure, at any particular level of economic activity, the community comprehensive effort may be able to reduce the influence of discrimination in employment and similar dysfunctions rooted in local economic behavior. But such undertakings are more realistically classed as inducing changes in the performance of local institutions than as dealing with the operation of the economy. There remain three avenues for intervention—the allocation of social resources, social adjustment, and the performance of local institutions.

There seems little question that the community can move, over a period of time, toward rectifying the maldistribution of social resources. One step would be the investment of substantial amounts of capital in transportation facilities, educational plant, housing development, and other types of redevelopment. Another would be the intensification of locally administered public services; for example, education, protection, and health, involving increased outlays for current expense. These undertakings have different dimensions; and, while they are interrelated as parts of a total action effort, they are not an administratively unified concern. Certainly they do not come within the scope of a sharply focussed program designed to reduce the incidence of urban poverty. The poverty program may mount modestly proportioned demonstration efforts to point the way to more comprehensive action, but apart from these the reallocation of social resources has to be recognized as an objective spanning a wide variety of activities, jurisdictions, and sectors of the urban area.

The community attack upon poverty, however, may generate interest and commitment to improve the allocation of social resources. Community leadership, drawn into active involvement in the anti-poverty program, may be sensitized by this experience to the deprivations resulting from a noxious social environment and may be stimulated to undertake remedial action. The involvement of the poor in the solution of their own problems could also have a dual effect. The poor, stimulated to move from latency to purposive expression, might put urgent pressure upon governing bodies to give greater attention to the needs of poverty areas. The same stimulus could contribute to the growth of cooperative self-help activities by the poor that would mitigate some of their difficulties. Altogether, the direct attack upon poverty and an improved distribution of social resources become counterpart, mutually reenforcing lines of action within the broad scope of urban problem-solving. Along with other activities they need to be drawn into the scope of a grand strategy of constructive urban action. From an operational point of view, each has its own programmatic characteristics.

The field of social adjustment seems better adapted to the capabilities of a community program. Broadly defined, this field includes all efforts at reinforcing the individual and his family in overcoming barriers to mobility, barriers evidenced by such difficulties as a lack of employability, limited literacy, and indications of a substantial range of social pathology. The emphasis is upon developing and reinforcing the capacity of the individual to participate and compete in the general society. So far as age and physical impairments forestall active competition, efforts are necessarily compensatory. These would be the objectives around which public, private, and voluntary activities could be mobilized in a comprehensive program involving the active participation of the poor. Designing and operating such an effort presents many difficulties, but the applicability of community action is not, so it would seem, a central difficulty. Community indifference, complacency, and preoccupation can retard the development of a fully adequate effort. The stimulus of Federal funding and the pressures of the activated poor may be needed to overcome civic inertia. Nevertheless, this is a path of intervention well suited to cooperative, comprehensive action in the urban area.

The performance of local institutions is another matter. Beyond question, deeply rooted behavior patterns discourage open housing, produce discrimination in employment, and limit educational opportunities for minority groups, particularly the non-white. It is difficult to attack these conditions directly by community action, especially where they are inadvertent and unconscious consequences of long established social stratification, but a direct attack may not be the most effective one. The comprehensive involvement of the community in reinforcing socio-economic mobility is a learning experience as well as an action process. The influences of institutional performance upon the mobility of the poor will become evident as the capacity for mobility is acquired. And, of course, these barriers are obvious targets for attack by the poor when they are stimulated toward self-help and self-improvement. In other words, institutional change may well come about as a by-product of the elimination of more specific and tangible barriers to mobility, rather than from attacks mounted against the institutions themselves.

In summary, the idea of community action would seem to be primarily applicable to efforts at stimulating and reinforcing the mobility of the poor so that their latent capabilities can be more effectively utilized toward their escape from poverty. Closely related is the lowering of barriers to mobility resulting from the way that institutions of the community tend to perpetuate the circumstances of poverty. It can be hoped that the momentum generated by these efforts will carry over to reinforce counterpart efforts to allocate the social resources of the community in a more equitable way.

This chapter has sketched the salient characteristics of three sets of considerations basic to a broad-aim, comprehensive attack upon a socio-economic problem, in this case urban poverty. The first is the nature of the basic problem, its causes and its attributes. No crisp, confident answers are forthcoming. A conclusion of indeterminacy is justified. Second, the urban area as the task environment is examined. Evident trends and capabilities, both fiscal and operational, are critical factors. Finally, community action as the framework for instrumental intervention is considered. The outcome is an estimate that intervention aimed in the first instance at social impairments limiting mobility is best adapted to community action. Stimulated by these efforts is change in the performance of local institutions where existing behavior tends to block mobility. Then further stimulation and reenforcement may be generated for a more functional allocation of the community's social resources. In this focus the next chapter takes up the design of a specific strategy of intervention aimed at building socio-economic mobility.

*Selected References*

The following references illustrate the type to which the generalist would turn for an initial grasp of a general problem. It should be recalled that the intent of the chapter is to suggest the framework of a broad-aim program. The characteristics pertinent to design of intervention are sketched, not fully developed as they would have to be in any specific task environment.

# SIMPLIFIED MODEL OF THE PROBLEM OF POVERTY
## IN RELATION TO COMMUNITY ACTION PROGRAM CAPABILITIES

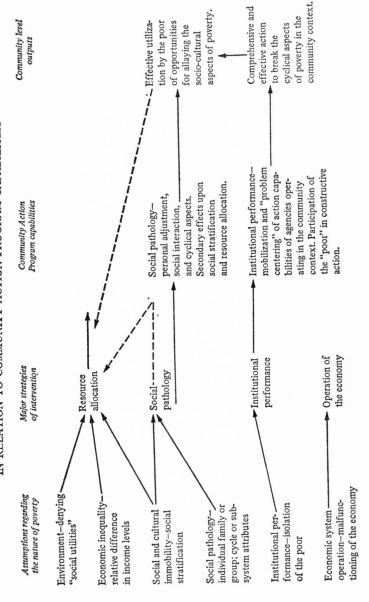

| *Assumptions regarding the nature of poverty* | *Major strategies of intervention* | *Community Action Program capabilities* | *Community level outputs* |
|---|---|---|---|
| Environment—denying "social utilities" | Resource allocation | | Effective utilization by the poor of opportunities for allaying the socio-cultural aspects of poverty. |
| Economic inequality—relative difference in income levels | | | |
| Social and cultural immobility—social stratification | Social-pathology | Social pathology—personal adjustment, social interaction, and cyclical aspects. Secondary effects upon social stratification and resource allocation. | Comprehensive and effective action to break the cyclical aspects of poverty in the community context. |
| Social pathology—individual family or group; cycle or sub-system attributes | | | |
| Institutional performance—isolation of the poor | Institutional performance | Institutional performance—mobilization and "problem centering" of action capabilities of agencies operating in the community context. Participation of the "poor" in constructive action. | |
| Economic system operation—malfunctioning of the economy | Operation of the economy | | |

James L. Sundquist's finding with respect to Federal aid investment in state and local problem-solving is from his *Making Federalism Work, A Study of Program Coordination at the Community Level* (with the collaboration of David W. Davis), The Brookings Institution, Washington, D. C., 1969. In *On Fighting Poverty*, edited by Sundquist and cited below, his chapter, "Origins of the War on Poverty," pp. 6–33, is valuable for background purposes. Robert S. Weiss and Martin Rein, in "The Evaluation of Broad-Aim Programs: Experimental Design, Its Difficulties and an Alternative," *Administrative Science Quarterly*, XV, 1 (March 1970), pp. 97–109, make perceptive use of the idea of broad-aim, broad-impact programs involving pervasive social change. The commentary by Donald T. Campbell, "Considering the Case against Experimental Evaluations of Social Innovations," ibid., pp. 110–113, should be considered along with the point of view of Weiss and Rein.

With respect to the nature of poverty and the community action strategy, a wide range of literature is now available. The summary statement of approaches to the understanding of poverty is based upon Martin Rein, "Social Science and the Elimination of Poverty," *Journal of the American Institute of Planners*, XXXIII, pp. 146–163 (May 1967). Especially valuable are S.M. Miller and Frank Riessman, *Social Class and Social Policy*, Basic Books, New York, 1968; Alvin Schnorr, *Explorations in Social Policy*, Basic Books, New York, 1968, especially chapter 17, "Policy Issues in Fighting Poverty," pp. 261–271; and Richard M. Titmus, *Commitment to Welfare*, Pantheon Books, Random House, New York, 1968. Michael Harrington's *The Other America*, MacMillan, New York, 1962, was, of course, a major influence in the development of the idea of a culture of poverty. More specifically applicable to the community action approach are Peter Marris and Martin Rein, *Dilemmas of Social Reform*, Atherton, New York, 1967, and Daniel P. Moynihan, *Maximum Feasible Misunderstanding, Community Action in the War on Poverty*, Macmillan-Free Press, New York, 1969. Two volumes of major importance are the products of the American Academy of Arts and Sciences, Seminar on Race and

Poverty. They are Daniel P. Moynihan (editor), *On Understanding Poverty, Perspectives from the Social Sciences*, Basic Books, New York, 1968; and James L. Sundquist (editor), *On Fighting Poverty, Perspectives From Experience*, Basic Books, New York, 1969.

The *Economic Opportunity Act of 1964* is 42 *United States Code Annotated* 2782 *et seq.*, PL 88–452, 78 Stat. 508, as amended.

In Paul F. Lazersfeld, William W. Sewell and Harold W. Wilensky (editors), *The Uses of Sociology*, Basic Books, New York, 1967, are several chapters especially valuable to the generalist. These are chapter 7, Henry J. Meyer, Eugene Litwak, Edwin J. Thomas and Robert D. Vinter, "Social Work and Social Welfare," pp. 156–190; chapter 16, Herbert L. Gans, "Urban Poverty and Social Planning," pp. 437–476; chapter 20, Harold W. Sheppard, "Unemployment, Manpower and Area Development," pp. 544–566; chapter 25, Thomas F. Pettigrew and Kurt W. Black, "Sociology in the Desegregation Process: Its Use and Disuse," pp. 692–722; and chapter 27, Herbert W. Wyman and Charles W. Wright, "Evaluating Social Action Programs," pp. 741–782.

With respect to the circumstances of urban areas, the literature is abundant. Especially useful materials are James Q. Wilson (editor), *The Metropolitan Enigma*, Chamber of Commerce of the United States, Washington, D. C., 1967; J. R. Meyer, J. F. Kain, and M. Wohl, *The Urban Transportation Problem*, Harvard, Cambridge, 1965, chapters 2–7, discussing economic change and urban location and their implications; and Warner Bloomberg, Jr. and Henry J. Schmandt (editors), *Power, Poverty, and Urban Policy*, Urban Affairs Annual Review, Vol. 2, Sage, Beverly Hills, 1968.

# II

# The Strategy of Intervention

AN EXPLORATORY ANALYSIS OF THE GENERALIZED problem of urban poverty suggests that the indicated target for a community action program is considerably narrower than the broad, and quite indeterminate, proportions of the problem as a whole. The target was the tangle of what may be termed social impairments or deprivations that limit the capacity of the poor to acquire the socio-economic mobility needed to move out of the condition of poverty. It was selected, not because on the available evidence a lack of mobility is clearly the most powerful influence producing poverty, although in many contexts it may well be, but because it holds the major probability for effective intervention through the means of a community action program. The result is that, for operating purposes, the problem has been reduced to a somewhat more manageable set of objectives and outcomes. The next stage of design is to consider what is involved in arriving at a specific strategy of intervention aimed at enabling the poor to use their capabilities freely and effectively to escape from entrapment in the condition of poverty.

It should be emphasized again that the purpose here is to

illustrate the process of problem factoring and intervention design so that instrumental efforts can be selected, interrelated, and balanced with substantial confidence that desired outcomes will be realized. Urban poverty is used to illustrate the complexities encountered where the objective is broad-aim and comprehensive impact.

Remedial intervention has to aim at tangible things to be done, definite changes to be made, manifest results to be produced. So the specific operating problem must be defined, the targets of intervention set, and the results, or changes to be induced, identified. This is to say that a series of questions must be asked and answered to arrive at a set of indicators as clear-cut and objective as possible. Where answers are elusive because verified knowledge is lacking or thin, as is often the case in the social fields, the gaps must be accommodated by exploratory strategies.

## Definition of the Problem

The design begins, of course with definition of the problem. In the simplest terms, this calls for three identifications: *first,* the field or context within which the problem is believed to exist; *second,* the desired state of affairs within this context; *third,* the observed existing state of affairs. The difference between the existing state and the desired state can be taken as the problem to be dealt with. For the first identification in any particular instance of urban poverty, various environmental and social indicators can be used to delineate the context in terms of physical area and population groups. City blocks or census tracts can designate areas showing blight, deteriorated housing, obsolete facilities, and the like. Within the area so designated, there would be, as disclosed by social and economic data, a relatively high concentration of assistance recipients, low income individuals and families, and the unemployed, and indications of social dysfunctions such as high rates of school dropout, juvenile delinquency, offenses against persons and property, personal injuries, and illness. These and other working criteria can be applied to describe a target area for intervention efforts.

The second identification is that of the desired state of affairs in the target area. What under optimal circumstances (as a condition of relative non-poverty) would be the characteristics of this area and the people living there? Here it should be emphasized that the ideas of a desired state of affairs and of optimal conditions are not expected to express ideal conditions. Working standards or criteria are intended, acceptable "pars" to characterize conditions amounting to an absence of poverty. Even this necessitates a choice of the attributes of poverty and non-poverty, which is to say the application of social values. The question of appropriate values will not be examined here. It is enough for present purposes to emphasize that a value choice is inevitable. So indeed it is in the definition of every program objective. No highway is expected to be accident-free. The control of infectious diseases ordinarily discounts some level of infection. A complete elimination of dysfunctions is rarely, if ever, expected. Always the question is, What is the acceptable and tolerable level of dysfunction beyond which expected benefits would not be justified by costs, however measured, or where available technical knowledge does not provide a workable basis for intervention?

The third identification is of the existing state of affairs in the target area. The area has been designated. The salient attributes have been identified and working "pars" have been set. The task is to intervene so that the circumstances of the target area and of its people move above the standards set as the working criteria. The next step in sharpening the statement of the problem is determining actual conditions within the target area, and measuring the degree of their relative salience by applying the marginal criteria applicable to them. This is more easily stated than accomplished; synthesis of the pertinent data and measurement of dysfunctions often are difficult. But it must be attempted though it may result only in a set of approximations. Obviously, if the general consensus is that intervention is urgently needed, the initiation or intensification of action cannot await precise understandings. But it must be designed and monitored to yield by feed-back the clarification of information without which intervention tends to be futile.

## Setting Priorities

When dysfunctions have been identified and measured against criteria of acceptable conditions, priorities must be considered. What is most important, most significant to do? What qualitatively are the most serious difficulties? What changes are critical in order to bring about at least an amelioration of poverty conditions? Answers to such questions as these rely upon the accumulated knowledge and experience of the relevant technical and professional disciplines. In this reliance, it is important to distinguish as clearly as possible between doctrine and conviction on the one hand, and hard knowledge and validated experience on the other.

It is equally important to distinguish between the causes of conditions regarded as dysfunctional, and their symptoms or attributes. The distinction is material whether or not the causes can be identified. Intervention to correct or eliminate causes is one thing; the amelioration of attributes is another. The elimination of causes is, of course, the major priority, and especially if there is reason for confidence that, once controlled, they will not reappear in some other form. But action directed at presumed root causes can leave an accumulation of attributes or symptoms that if ignored can become causes in themselves. Thus a two-fold strategy has to be considered. On the one side basic causes are attacked and eliminated so far as available knowledge and technology permit. On the other, consequences must be alleviated. Yet a strategy of action aimed only at amelioration is likely to be ineffective because the basic causes continue to produce the conditions that intervention seeks to alleviate. This observation seems self-evident, but the tendency is to invest much more heavily in ameliorating adverse conditions than in seeking out and correcting their causes. Meanwhile causes continue unabated to produce the characteristic dysfunctions; ameliorative action churns along seeking to compensate for the basic problems without coming to grips with them. The ongoing workload of compensatory action grows in bulk but seldom in effectiveness.

## The Action Strategy

When action priorities are set, with some set of major basic causes to be eliminated and serious consequences to be alleviated, the next consideration is the means of instrumental intervention. Instrumental capabilities, particularly in the social fields, by no means match the appetite for problem solving in the public sector. By and large, methods of intervention are still blunt, clumsy, and only approximate. The margin of error is far too great. Because little is known in any precise way about cause-effect relationships, the development of intervention techniques to eliminate cause has lagged.

But some battery of instrumental techniques must be chosen. These techniques are in large part the special properties, indeed the status symbols, of various technical and professional groups in the society. For all practical purposes, however, and especially in the relatively short run, there is no feasible alternative to relying upon them in designing public problem-solving intervention. In the longer run special administrative technologies, and disciplines embodying them, may develop in the public sector. Forest management, highway engineering, and arid land reclamation are prominent examples. But the available instrumental "know-how" of the society and economy generally amounts to the tool-kit upon which public intervention has to rely. Thus the questions are, What do we know how to do? and How can it be applied in one or another mix to produce change-inducing influences upon the causes and consequences of poverty? A good deal can be said, and will be taken up later, about approaches to answering these questions. The scanning of all applicable modes of action, the factoring of alternative combinations of activity, and the evaluation of internal balance and consistency come into play.

The availability of resources to support action is another important question. The availability of developed instrumental skills is one aspect of this concern. Another and most urgent aspect has to do with optimizing the use of scarce resources. Legal authority is in point because every grant of capacity to act is implicitly limited by its terms, by interrelated legislation, by the constitutional framework, and by remedies available to those who regard action as unreasonable, arbitrary, or capricious. Funding is often scanty; financial resources must be managed in accordance with statutory requirements. In short, resources are invariably limited in variety and total amount, and there are constraints upon the uses to which they can be put. The pattern of resources investment should be designed to optimize the impact of the program effort.

A further aspect of the action strategy is the projection of the rate and quality level of the production of the change-inducing influences. As will be explained later in connection with program design, this involves the entire network of end products (change influences), component programs, and intermediate activities. For each element of action, characteristics and rates of production must be projected. Unless this is done there is no basis for the interpretation and evaluation of feedback information. The difficult questions of measurement and quality standards are involved. But altogether, the evaluation of the effectiveness of an intervention effort is next to impossible unless the expected impacts are projected and scheduled at least experimentally, and the component activities intended to cumulate in these impacts are set in a disciplined framework. Otherwise, activities easily become randomized, often compulsive, responses to perceived urgencies, and there is little basis for judgment upon whether any intended difference has been accomplished.

## Urban Poverty

This treatment of the essentials of a strategy of intervention is neither complete in scope nor exhaustive in depth. But it serves its purpose if it sets a working framework for the design of an intervention strategy to deal with the condition of poverty in the urban setting. It is now necessary to arrive at a working concept of the way social impairments relate to urban poverty, a set of ideas around which an intervention strategy can be built. The exploratory efforts undertaken in the preceding chapter do not lead to any crisp, specific identification of primary causes or controlling attributes. An effort to come to grips with the resulting difficulties might start with some such formulation as this. Poverty may be conceptualized as a lack of effective socioeconomic interaction with the society as a whole. It may be regarded as a kind of isolation resulting in an inability to maintain the interactions that, it is ordinarily assumed, contribute to social and economic self-sufficiency, mobility, self-realization, and the like. This lack of interaction would appear to be rooted in some mix of causative influences. Primary among these would seem to be an inhibiting social and physical environment, economic inequality in the sense that the poor seem clustered at the lower end of the range of income distribution, sociocultural immobility in that stratification inhibits movement out of poverty circumstances, particularly in the case of the non-white poor, social maladjustment and pathology that impair productive societal interaction, and the tendency of critical institutions of the society to perform in a way that rather reinforces than mitigates tendencies toward isolation and non-interaction. This is not an easy concept to operationalize. About all that can be said is that intervention seeks to build a capacity among the poor for effective socio-economic interaction, effective in the sense that mobility is acquired, and seeks also to lower the barriers to effective interaction.

The task is to operationalize these objectives in the urban area, recognizing the presence and the force of a galaxy of troublesome constraints. A direct attack upon a noxious environment is hardly a short-range undertaking, and it is not clear that environment, as such, is a controlling cause. Economic inequality can be compensated for effectively only by nation-wide policies that underpin the economic status of the lowest income groups. Barriers to mobility rooted in socio-economic stratification do not appear to be subject to direct and specific intervention efforts. Probably these barriers will be reduced when the groups now isolated develop and exercise a capacity to interact productively in the society as a whole. Thus in the urban context it would seem that specific objectives for intervention need to be built around at least two primary purposes. The first is to deal in preventive and remedial ways with accumulated impairments to interaction. The second is to reorient the performance of institutions that are failing to contribute effectively to building mobility on the part of the poor.

In developing an action strategy to deal with barriers to effective socioeconomic interaction, a first step is to ask whether the individual, the family group, or the social collectivity develop characteristics or attributes that in themselves limit and impair effective utilization of opportunities for mobility. The literature of the field indicates that such characteristics may develop. It appears that at least three types of operating assumptions are available; others may be regarded as variations of the primary approaches. The design of intervention effort, then, can begin with an exploration of these operating assumptions with the objective of determining the points of intervention they assume to be critical, and the consequences that intervention can be expected to produce. These assumptions can be differentiated for purposes of explanation by the "level" to which each applies. The first emphasizes the personal or individual level; the second, the socio-cultural; the third, a societal or subcultural system. Like most labels, these involve a considerable simplification. Whatever approach, or combination of them, is taken as a point of departure, working assumptions tend to converge into a limited range of available action channels.

The first type of operating approach can be identified with and directed at the problems of personal growth and adjustment. The underlying assumption is that the capacity of the individual to function effectively in the society depends upon how well transitions are made at critical points in the life cycle. These transitions or turning points may be pre-school to school, school to economic competition, individual to family responsibility, and economic productivity to post workforce status. These illustrations are only approximate; obviously there can be many critical points in the life span when the roles and role requirements of the individual change. The working assumption is that at each turning point significant adjustments must be made if the transition is to be functional; a failure can produce incapacities to use personal capabilities effectively in societal interactions. Failure may be attributable to impediments, singly or in combination, inhering in the individual, the family or group context, the physical environment, or the social or economic ecology. A failure at one transition point may impair an individual's capacity to make functional adjustments at subsequent points in his life span.

Under assumptions of this type, intervention aims at (1) reinforcing the individual at the critical turning points, (2) compensating for a failure or incapacity to accommodate at previous turning points in his life, (3) mitigating the influences external to the individual that make successful adjustment difficult or impossible.

In the general category of sociocultural assumptions, the idea of the cycle of poverty is dominant. Indeed the orientation implicit in this point of view dominates much of the War on Poverty. In oversimplified terms, the idea is that the attributes of poverty tend to perpetuate themselves and, over time, become causes in themselves. Poverty once rooted in the society produces conditions that breed poverty. For example, the poor tend to cluster in slum environments because lack of income, racial segregation, and like influences force them into such housing circumstances and foreclose alternative choices. The slum environment then produces dysfunctional attributes among the people caught there, and these attributes tend to impair mobility. In this approach significance is attributed to forces external to the individual and the family as the influences causing and perpetuating poverty. But these external influences produce human impairments that are separately transmitted and maintained. For present purposes, the plausibility of this set of assumptions need not be evaluated. The implicit socio-economic determinism underlying the approach is the subject of earnest debate. Here it is enough to take notice of the salience of the ideas in framing strategies of intervention.

Remedial action based upon this view of poverty aims at breaking the cycle at as many points as possible; the breaking of the cycle permits escape. Because basic causes and acquired attributes resulting from exposure to poverty are interlocked, a broadly proportioned, even random strategy of intervention is acceptable. Targets of opportunity are as effective as pin-pointed remedial steps. Given sufficient resources, the breaking up of ghettos, the development of broader employment, the stimulation of motivation and aspiration, the encouragement of self-organization and of problem-solving efforts can be counted upon to build toward a cumulative effect.

The idea of powerlessness on the part of the poor has a bearing upon the breaking of the cycle of poverty. The assumption would seem to be that a strong influence toward perpetuating the cycle is the lack of perceived advantage in breaking it to the dominant power groups in the society. If the poor can accumulate a capacity to exercise power in their own behalf, they will move to break the cycle. If the poor can influence public policy formation and administration to respond positively to their demands, public action breaking the cycle will ensue, enabling the poor to move out of entrapment and to function in a more benign context.

A third set of working assumptions uses a societal or sub-cultural point of view. Ideas derived from systems theory model the general society as an essentially open system, characterized by drives toward self and group realization, value expression, status mobility, and the like. Varieties of inputs are converted into the social energy that gives the system vitality and productivity. The outputs are in the forms of satisfactions, experienced or anticipated, and these satisfactions generate the fresh inputs of social energy that assure the system continuity through time. A pattern of subsystems interact as components of the general societal system; each has its own special characteristics and functions. One of these is the subsystem of poverty.

Of the subsystems in this formulation, that of poverty is distinctive because it is a relatively closed system. It is maintained by inputs from the general societal system, and from its subsystems, in the nature of socioeconomic components that do not function effectively in the dynamic interactions of high energy systems. The inputs, in this sense, are low energy inputs. They tend to maintain a low energy subsystem, sluggish and indifferent, with little capacity to produce expressive outputs. Whatever outputs it can produce have little, if any, functional utility in the operation of the higher energy systems. To put the point a bit differently, the inputs of the poverty subsystem are mainly "spin-offs" from the larger system. Socioeconomic components of submarginal utility tend to be rejected because they do not contribute effectively to the input-throughput-output process of the general society. These rejected components cluster in a low energy subsystem of interaction patterns aimed mainly at generating sufficient energy to maintain the subsystem in a noxious environment. The rejected "spin-offs" of the larger systems are such entities as blighted physical environment, obsolete kinds of employment, submarginal productive skills, human groups culturally blocked from high energy interaction, and so forth.

This sketch of a possible systems model is neither fully developed or theoretically explained. The purpose is only to identify the approach so that a course of intervention developed around its assumptions can be understood in comparison with intervention projected from other sets of assumptions. Such a course of intervention would be directed toward (1) closing off the specific inputs judged most active in the immediate context, (2) opening up channels for escape from the low energy subsystem, and (3) accelerating the natural process of entropy by eliminating so far as possible the social and economic influences in which the subsystem has its roots. These steps taken, the subsystem of poverty can be expected to die of attrition because of a lack of energy inputs and environmental supports. The special characteristic of this approach is that it calls for a much more selective, a considerably more discrete set of interventions than does the cycle of poverty model. Analysis is required in each specific context to identify the more effective inputs to the subsystem and the factors that sustain it. Also, the points of potential linkage, of output to the larger societal systems, need identification so that tendencies toward closure can be overcome. The strategy of intervention would be built around the results of these analyses.

Thus the problem of poverty as a cluster of socioeconomic phenomena can be approached by using experimental assumptions of at least three types—the personal, the sociocultural, and the societal subsystem. Again it must be emphasized that all these are working assumptions; none have been validated empirically. Indeed, and this is a most important consideration, it is entirely possible in a particular context to design a battery of intervention instruments that would satisfy the assumptions of all three models with little incompatibility. The consequences of the uses of these instruments would be additive and cumulative rather than self-cancelling. This done, a principle of equifinality can be said to be invoked. Whatever validity each of the approaches may have, and whatever they have in gross, will be utilized without risking the possibility of a hard choice of reliance upon one to the exclusion of the others. A strategy of intervention encompassing the range of plausible assumptions renders differences among them immaterial.

## Differential Change

Intervention to reduce the incidence of poverty essentially aims at inducing change. A comprehensive anti-poverty strategy undertakes to produce several kinds of change, whatever the operating assumptions about the causes of poverty and the critical objectives at which specific efforts at intervention are directed. Change, it can be assumed, is sought in employment opportunities, in the physical environment in which the poor live, and in the opportunities available to them to improve their circumstances. Change in the capabilities of the poor to utilize opportunities is also important. Literacy and skills are needed to compete for employment. Impairments, whether physical or social in nature, need to be overcome or compensated for. It is assumed that aspirations need to be stimulated and reinforcements supplied toward realizing them. Altogether, these efforts add up to assuring greater mobility, indeed a guided mobility, enabling the poor to move out of the conditions of poverty into a full and effective interaction in the economy and the society as a whole. This also involves change in the way the institutions of the community function. Public education, social welfare, health care, employment and training organizations require a reorientation to bring their potential contributions into productive participation. So the questions arise as to the nature of the changes that are being sought and the relative ease or difficulty to be expected in realizing them.

Clearly change can be of several types, and of several degrees of difficulty. To illustrate the point, a very rough and tentative classification will be suggested. For present purposes, types of change may be seen as systemic, cognitive, and affective; each has its own characteristics and requirements. Systemic change, in this connection, means the reordering, rephasing, or elaboration of the components of an existing action process. For example, the intensification of existing municipal services in a poverty area would be this type of change. So also would be the decentralization of service locations to improve their availability to the poor. In such instances, the existing and learned repertory of operating behaviors would remain substantially unchanged. Very little relearning or reorientation would be involved. Awkward and dysfunctional aspects of the activity systems would be changed with a view to reducing barriers to operating effectiveness. This is the simplest and the easiest type of change, and it is also the one most likely to be effective over a relatively short period.

Cognitive change is more difficult, unless of course the predisposition to cognitive readjustment already exists and needs only reinforcement to become operational. As used here, the idea of cognitive change is that of a difference in the patterns of perception controlling the behavior responses of the groups participating in the action process. It is assumed that stimuli of one variety or another, often well learned and even stereotyped, evoke learned response patterns. An employable person is a cluster of attributes which have become associated with the condition of employment. When these attributes are perceived, the action process linking the person with job opportunity functions. If they are not perceived, the action process is not evoked. This formulation can be applied to the educable child, the trainable adult, the responsible credit risk, and so on. Limited and stereotyped cognition tends to immobilize action; program innovation often is basically the reorientation of cognitive patterns. Available skills and operating techniques are brought to bear upon problems previously bypassed because of cognitive limitations.

What happens is that the range of perceived stimuli evoking

action is broadened, and already available response patterns are applied toward problem solving. Illustrations come to mind. In the recent past, public employment services have been undergoing induced change from a labor demand orientation to a labor supply emphasis. Previously the effort was to find qualified persons to fill available vacancies in private employment. The newer approach is to develop placements for persons seeking employment. Some systemic change is involved but this is not significant in comparison with cognitive changes occasioned by the shift to the labor supply orientation. Another example is in the orientation of the social service agencies that in many communities have centered their attention upon the so-called middle class families. The poor, and especially the non-white poor, have been outside the cognitive pattern.

The idea of affective change, as used here, identifies the alteration of subsumed value orientations. It seems safe to assume that nearly all fields of activity, whatever their nature, are marked by sets of values, often subtle and so generally accepted that social dysfunctions resulting from them escape notice. The familiar ideas of the cooperative and appreciative patient, the motivated employee, the involved student, and the like, connote expectations on the part of the groups administering the services involved, and these expectations in turn appear to express the values practitioners place upon their special social roles. Clients who respond by a sharing of these values, or who in other respects match the practitioner's expectations, contribute to a kind of rapport that induces the exchange of social energy between client and practitioner. The counterpart circumstance is also observed. The essentially interpersonal relationship just illustrated projects into group and collectivity interactions. Thus cultural and subcultural differences obvious in personal appearance can become blocks to socio-economic mobility. Presumed attributes of personal reliability and capability are attached, with little rationality but often with strong social re-inforcement, to race, income level, area of residence, style of speech, and other characteristics. These biases often become part of the structured value patterns that limit and condition both socio-economic mobility and the response capabilities of institutionalized groups.

In any particular set of circumstances, these three types of change are likely to be interrelated. A long established operating system develops set cognitive patterns; action patterns become frozen; and deeply rooted values grow around roles and identities in the ongoing system. It is rare to encounter the simple situation in which only one type of change is indicated to produce a desired consequence. In instances where systemic adjustment can be undertaken without involving significant cognitive or affective variables, change can take the form of system elaboration, sometimes a release from annoying constraints. In such instances, increased funding and the addition of professional staff can contribute to a desired reorientation of action. But cognitive change is more difficult, unless differential and more functional perceptions are latent, or denied expression because of constraints limiting the range of system responses to perceived stimuli. Where a restructuring of cognitive patterns is indicated, two kinds of strategies suggest themselves. If relatively rapid transition is not urgent, a strategy of reeducation can be undertaken. Indeed in many instances there is no practical alternative. The process is usually slow and full of risks. If relatively rapid change is essential, about the only option is innovation using an *ad hoc* organization starting afresh. This is also a gamble. If it succeeds, the educative ripple-effect can be highly profitable; if it fails, the new perceptions can be rejected as wholly worthless. Affective change is the most difficult and time consuming of all. Invariably an existing value structure embodies sunk social costs, perceptions of identities and statuses, and assumptions of limited, even distorted reality. Change is slow, difficult, and hazardous because of the emotional, nonrational elements rooted in the belief structure. The complexities are such that the problem of affective change in a community-wide value structure cannot be explored here. Where the problem is centered in an operating agency, the most effective approach would seem to be the "wither-on-the vine" technique. In terms of social costs, the least expensive approach may be to initiate a wholly new program operation, bypassing and isolating the presently ineffective effort. The organization components thus rendered obsolete are reduced to a token existence, and the fresh effort built to major effectiveness. But the innovating effort must be built as a total system operating in a relatively benign environment of public reinforcement. This may not be easy to develop.

## The Question of Determinacy

A set of further considerations enters into any design of intervention, whether the field is the production of intangible social products such as change-inducing influences, or more tangible consequences such as fire protection or highway facilities. These considerations may be characterized as relating to the degree of determinacy, or indeterminacy, associated with the outcomes of projected action. Program activity can be regarded as relatively determinate when the outcome of action is predictable within reasonably narrow limits. The result of mass inoculation against infectious disease, for example, can be counted upon to be the reduction of the incidence of such illness by some substantial degree. On the other hand, the outcome may be quite indeterminate. Vocational training of an unskilled person may increase his potential for competition in the labor force. But it does not assure that he will be an economically self-sufficient person because there are independent variables influencing the desired outcome which are not directly controlled by the development of job skills. Beyond this simple illustration, moreover, there are often factors of such incomplete knowledge of cause-effect relationships, and of imprecise operating methods, that the outcomes of intervention can be only problematical within a rather wide range of possibilities. A reasonably realistic way to view available intervention techniques in any particular instance is to see them along a range reaching from determinate outcomes at one extreme to entirely indeterminate outcomes at the other. Risk, of course, is minimized, other factors remaining equal, by relying upon relatively determinate means. But in the social fields such an approach is difficult because determinate intervention is seldom possible; and, in the case of poverty, outcomes are thoroughly speculative. The risk of unexpected, undesired, dysfunctional outcomes at the present state of knowledge is disconcertingly high.

Every strategy of intervention is grounded in some set of assumptions about cause-effect relationships. These assumptions, derived from developed and validated knowledge, accumulated operating experience, or sometimes only a kind of dogma, are at the core of the operating design. It is assumed that some pattern of action flows using more or less disciplined administrative behaviors can be linked together so as to maximize the probability of realizing desired outcomes, and minimize the possibility of contributing to undesired results. But the state of knowledge about the reliability of these causal relationships is a critical matter. Especially is this the case when the structure of program action involves the production of a mix of intermediate products, which may themselves be intangible. Uncertainty increases when this mix is projected along with other product combinations to add up to a program component intended to exert a desired change influence. As working assumptions are projected from stage to stage of such an intervention design, the element of risk of course is magnified.

*Variable Constraints*

There are other variables influencing the likelihood of realizing desired outcomes. In any design of intervention, some pattern of constraints is assumed. At any one time each of these constraints may be relatively active or substantially latent. Among the active ones, the combination of positive or supporting influences and negative or restraining pressures often contributes to a kind of ongoing homeostasis in the program effort. But there is nothing stable about this interaction. The relative energy exerted by active constraints can and does change, and latent constraints can become more active. The capacity of the program effort to maintain a steady state of disciplined, channeled activity is subjected to severe strains. The capacity for maintaining a structured, carefully designed strategy of action, particularly in a new agency or in a new cooperative combination of agencies, is probably marginal at best. The effectiveness of organic homeostasis in a program undertaking may well be a function of acquired maturity. Moreover, some advanced degree of maturity is probably essential to the capacity to live through contingencies—the unexpected, unpredictable, even cataclysmic events that threaten continued existence.

A strategy of intervention aimed at the alleviation of poverty is open to the disturbing influences of indeterminate intermediate outcomes, the erratic behavior of constraints, and the impact of dramatic contingencies. The probability of dysfunctional consequences and of disrupting influences must be discounted in projecting the design of intervention. There are limited means for coping with these eventualities which can be built into the action design. Because these are more appropriately factors of program design, they will be considered in the next chapter.

Altogether, the design of a strategy of intervention dealing with poverty, and for that matter any intervention in the complex social fields, has to encompass a set of essentials. The problem must be identified and defined, at least sufficiently to provide a point of departure and a framework for the testing and refining of operating assumptions. The targets for intervention must be set and the methods of intervention must be realistically operational. These requirements assume some pattern of essentially theoretical assumptions about why the problem exists, and what action will make a justified difference in the incidence of the problem and in the consequences of the problem's persistence. Where alternative sets of assumptions are available with no validated basis for choice among them, a strategy of equifinality may be possible, proceeding along a path of incremental steps reinforced by feedback analysis. Then, it is essential to recognize that change itself is differential in nature. Simple systemic change is favored wherever it is applicable. Cognitive change is slower and more difficult. Affective change is the most difficult. Finally, it is impossible to avoid the problematical nature of cause-effect assumptions that enter into the design of intervention in a field such as poverty. The possibility of unexpected and dysfunctional consequences is substantial. Such is the challenge confronting the designer of intervention.

*Selected References*

An example of a reconnaissance study of the task environment is chapter II, *Research Report No. 1, Final Report, Social Change Evaluation Project*, University of Washington, Seattle, 1969, 21–57.

The three operating approaches for dealing with barriers to effective socio-economic interaction were developed in discussions of the Project Steering Committee. The idea of equifinality is familiar in systems theory.

## SIMPLIFIED MODEL OF INSTRUMENTAL INTERVENTION
## IN THE SOCIO-CULTURAL ASPECTS OF POVERTY

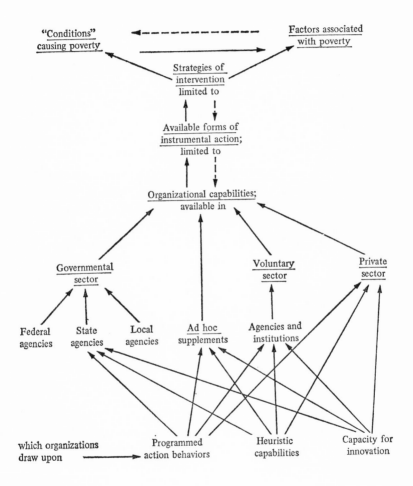

Direct action relationships_____

Indirect or secondary relationships_ _ _ _ _ _ _ _ _ _

The classification of types of change was developed for the purpose of emphasizing differential responses to change stimuli as these stimuli are perceived by the subjects of change.

A very useful volume which appeared since this study was undertaken is Alfred J. Kahn, *Theory and Practice of Social Planning*, Russell Sage Foundation, New York, 1969.

# III

# The Program System:
# Operating Program Design

THE OPERATING PROGRAM IMPLEMENTS THE STRA-tegy of intervention. It is the stage at which the design aimed at generating and expressing change in the community is developed into a structure of action. The productive capabilities possessed by the various operating agencies in all sectors of the community's life are marshalled into rationally designed patterns of action geared to the output of change-inducing influences. Activity flows interrelated and time-phased, interdependent and balanced, are projected, culminating in the outputs required by the intervention strategy. Coordinating and unifying influences are necessary; these are also designed and applied as a cohering overlay upon the action structure.

In this chapter the elements of this design will be explained and illustrated in a briefly sketched experimental model. The working assumptions are recalled. Then the action system approach is summarized. An illustrative model of an action system is developed to show how total change impact can be factored into major areas of productive effort. Each of these areas breaks into action components, and each component into a cluster of productive activities. Various agencies are allocated roles as producers of the social products that are the building blocks in the comprehensive structure of action. Thus the structure is one of action rather than of organizations. Participating agencies contribute their intermediate or component products to the general system of community action. The needs for unity and coherence in the operation of the system are supplied by a network of contractual agreements, an information system, and a public liaison system. The function of strategic control is essential; it will be developed in the next chapter.

*The Framework*

Several working assumptions should be recalled before design of the operating program is illustrated. The community action program would emphasize, as feasible objectives for the relatively short term, the reduction of social pathology among the poor, and the reinforcement of their socio-economic mobility. The institutions and organizations of the community in all sectors—public, private, and voluntary—would be mobilized in a comprehensive effort to provide needed services to the poor and to reduce barriers to needed mobility. The latter objective is two-fold. Invoking the productive capabilities of the community as a whole would maximize operating resources. The hope was that their positive involvement would also modify accumulated attitudes, habit patterns, and operating practices discriminating against the poor, and especially the non-white poor. The present and potential producers of services and change-inducing influences in the community have been identified, and their capabilities evaluated.

For purposes of illustration, it is further assumed that the targets for concentrated effort have been selected. The extent of poverty, the characteristics of the poor, and the reasons for poverty in these areas are known only in a very general way. It is estimated that the poor have little social organization or sensitivity to communication. The general educational level is distinctly lower than for the community as a whole. Drop-out rates in secondary education are high. Employable persons are regarded as low skilled and under employed. Arrest rates for minor offenses are high. On the basis of this thin and limited information, the intervention strategy amounts to a combination of increased educational accomplishment, a higher level of employability, and a reduction in social, especially family, disorganization. To stimulate stronger motivation toward mobility and to involve the poor in constructive efforts, community activities will be employed.

## The Action System Approach

The theoretical ideas underlying the action system approach should be sketched before illustrating the design of the operating program in this framework. A pattern of ideas basic to the general systems approach is used to express a working model of program action. Community action falls into the general class of sociocultural, as distinct from physical or biological, systems. The interacting components are social entities, social organisms, and communication linkages. Constraints, contingencies, and other variable factors are social forces. The energy exchanged with the external context and processed by the action system is social energy.

The community context is viewed as a complex of sociocultural systems that are "natural," as distinct from being designed and administered. The community itself is seen as less than a developed system. But it usually shows some degree of systems attributes. The tendency of more fully developed systems to assume structured roles in system interaction, a reliance upon identifiable communications linkages, and a tendency toward a steady state in system interrelationships are examples. The pattern of natural systems provides a tendency toward a structuring of value dispositions, cognitive patterns, and goal structures. Thus within the scope of this natural system context, a capacity for cooperative individual and group behavior develops with respect to some concerns, and immobilizing conflict develops with respect to others. The resulting "natural" system complex is the base upon which designed and administered systems become overlays. Systemic action amounts to continuing interchanges of energy between the natural and the designed systems functioning in a shared environment.

The action system is in the category of the designed and administered system. It is calculated to mobilize and interrelate a set of productive capabilities in various agencies and formal organizations toward the production of certain desired consequences in the environment. In some instances its system attributes may be less than complete and mature. In these cases system stability, to the extent that it is realized, is contributed by the properties of the more mature component subsystems. The action system is actually a structure of subsystems, each with its own attributes and properties. The structure as a whole is linked together both by formal (designed) and informal (natural) exchanges, primarily of information and energy. The action system is purposive. It has goals to fulfill, objectives to accomplish. Expectations held by internal groups and external collectivities need to be satisfied by the operation of the system so that fresh energy will be generated and fed into the system by the expectation of further satisfactions to be experienced in the future. The action system shows the properties and characteristics of designed systems. It has components, it processes energy in an input-throughout-output process, it uses feedback loops to communicate information to points of control and adjustment, it has tendencies toward maintaining a steady state, and it is subject to entropy.

## The Modeled Action System

The structural and process characteristics of the action system should now be pulled together to convey a general view of the way the modified system is expected to function. For this purpose it is useful to begin with the idea of the system's purpose as expressed in its output and impact. Then the structured process for producing the components of output will be traced.

Socio-economic change is the purpose of a community action program designed to deal with the condition of poverty. This change has two aspects. One is more effective interaction between the poor and other segments of the community, leading to the results of economic self-sufficiency for individuals and families, a more benign social and physical environment, reduced social pathology and maladjustment, and the like. The other aspect is in the performance of community institutions and agencies. As is usually the case with efforts at socio-economic change, the impact does not appear to result directly from intervention. Rather, the intervention action program produces change-inducing influences which in turn are expected to generate the sought-for change. It is change-inducing influences that are the outputs of the program system, the products of its productive activities. As such they are usually intangible social products. Their consequences sometimes are, and sometimes are not, identifiable and measurable. Objective evidences of program effort and activity usually are seen only at earlier stages of the production process.

For modelling purposes, total program output can be factored into major program areas. These do not represent discrete, mutually exclusive areas of change; they are interacting and mutually reinforcing. Their differentiation as program areas derives rather from operating characteristics than ultimate consequences. A program area incorporates a cluster of program components. Each component is identified with a sub-objective contributing to the wholeness of the program area, and is made up of a set of activities undertaken in most instances by several operating agencies. It is worth special note that the ongoing activities of formal organizations enter this pattern as producers of activity elements, and that linkages of formal organizational authority among them are not necessary. Other types of interties can be effective and are more functional in mobilizing the productive resources of the community as a whole.

The program as a whole can be sketched, for purposes of illustration, in terms of the four sets of change-inducing influences suggested as best calculated to produce the indicated changes among the people and groups defined as the poor. These become the major program areas: enhanced educational accomplishment, more effective participation in the labor force, the amelioration of the social problems of the poor, and the stimulation of self-help action on the part of the poor both to utilize available reinforcing services and to exercise initiative in the solving of personal, family, and sub-community problems that the operating program does not reach directly.

*Education.* The objective of the program area of education is increased educational accomplishment. Three major program components are selected: school readiness, sustained educational accomplishment, and adult literacy. Each one has its special operating activities. School readiness, for example, relies primarily upon Head Start child development, carried on by a number of groups, variously sponsored, in selected locations throughout the target areas. Other pre-school activities are geared to the specialized needs of particular groups of children, or to family needs for day care and supervision to enable the mother to undertake employment. The sustained educational accomplishment component is aimed at the reinforcement of the pupil so that educational development occurs at a normal pace and drop-outs are avoided. Possible activities would be primary and secondary level tutoring groups adapted to the special problems and needs of children who show difficulty in maintaining an expected rate of educational development. These groups also might be variously sponsored and located throughout the target areas. The adult literacy component is intended to assist persons beyond school age in overcoming inadequacies in basic education, inadequacies that can produce obstacles to desired socio-economic mobility. Here again the pattern of specific activities would be built around the identified needs of people in the target population, the availability of facilities, and the capabilities of sponsoring agencies. This sketch of structure leaves many questions unanswered. What sponsoring agencies, delegate agencies are to be selected? Which can be regarded as most productive? How is the relative volume of activity of the program components to be projected, authorized, and balanced? How are measures of productivity and effectiveness to be developed and applied so that the return upon the investment of resources can be optimized? These questions are pertinent and significant, and will be considered when the elements of program structure have been explained.

*Employment.* The objective, more effective participation in the labor force, identifies the employment program area. Three program components are emphasized. The first, training and placement, undertakes to develop job skills and capabilities and to place trainees in productive employment. Two sets of agency activities contribute. One is engaged in training for industrial employment and for the use of similar skills in repair and maintenance service; the other, with training for employment as paraprofessionals, particularly in the health care services. These two employment areas are assumed, for purposes of illustration, to have the best opportunities for the utilization of developed job knowledge and skills in the community. Another program component is employment counselling and referral. This is for persons already having necessary job qualifications, whose need is for referral to employment opportunities, guidance to prospective employers providing supportive employment environments, and counseling with respect to conduct on the job and relationships with supervisors and fellow employees. A third program component can be termed developmental experience. The aim is to develop in the individual an understanding of the context of employment, the responsibilities of regular attendance and effort, and the need for reliability in on-the-job behavior. A "sheltered" employment arrangement might be used. Delegate agencies might provide the work experience, intended frankly to condition persons for effective competition in the world of work. The sheltered employment would be designed as developmental and short-term. The employee would be "spun-off" into the general employment market as soon as he is regarded as ready for self-sufficiency. The activities in this employment program area could, and no doubt would, be undertaken by various delegate agencies, their responsibilities assigned according to the specialized service each provides, or by the geographical area within which it operates. The productive capabilities would be interrelated in a designed pattern of program contributions. The important point is that the program area as a whole is designed to satisfy the criteria of meeting the more intense needs, expressing a clear sense of priorities, and maintaining balance among interrelated needs.

*Social Adjustment.* The change-inducing influences undertaking to ameliorate the social problems of the poor cluster in

a program area characterized for convenience as social adjustment. Program components would depend, of course, upon the
characteristics and needs of the target population. Five are used
here to illustrate the design of the program area. A first and
rather obvious one is better utilization of available social services, the premise being that the poor have little understanding
of the availability of these services, and little information about
using them. The activities of this program component identify
particularized needs, refer persons to the service-providing
agencies, and maintain contact with the case to determine the
outcome of referral and to make supplementary referrals if
indicated. This is a coordinated referral service, spanning available resources in the community. Referrals are not limited
to the agencies directly participating in the community program but extend to all those with a capability to contribute to
problem solution in the individual case instance.

Other program components are more specific. Meeting the
poor's needs for legal counsel is one of these. Usually at least
one, and sometimes more than one, provider of such services
will be available. Counsel in civil matters is often different from
and separately administered from representation in criminal
cases. Probation services may be important. It has been assumed
that the target population shows a relatively high incidence of
prosecutions for minor offenses. Jail sentences have little constructive utility; probation services, so it appears, can make a
positive contribution. Cases coming under supervision through
this channel also may have characteristics that justify referral
to other social agencies. These implications are important.

The problem of the aging is an aspect of social adjustment.
Persons out of the employment market because of age, and
with very limited income, represent an important segment of
the poor. The service appropriate to their special circumstances
need not be reviewed here. It is enough to note that a subsistence

income is often not sufficient for subsistence, especially in the urban setting. Another program component, also a family service, might be family planning, planned parenthood. Illustrations could be multiplied. In any particular target area, the characteristics of the poor, and their needs for reinforcement in social adjustment can be identified. The supporting resources of the community can be mobilized toward meeting these needs. The design of a program area with this objective has its problems, and they will be considered later.

*Self-help Action.* The fourth set of change-inducing influences seek to stimulate the poor to identify and meet their own individual and group needs. This can be designated a program area of self-help action. Two program components are illustrative of the characteristics of such action. For one, organized self-help groups rely upon neighborhood organizations to stimulate functional interaction among persons and families toward identification of shared needs, cooperative efforts at problem-solving, and joint action in seeking and utilizing assisting services. An important aspect of this approach is its attempt to overcome the assumed tendencies of the poor toward latency, passivity, and withdrawal. Also it is intended to stimulate a learning process in the use of social energy toward opening up channels for socio-economic mobility. The risks involved in strategies of this sort are obvious. There is no assurance that the neighborhood action so stimulated will be functional in terms of high priority needs, that it will result in positive cooperation rather than disruptive conflict, or in identification with the larger community rather than introverted withdrawal. A further risk is that unrealistic expectations for rapid change can be generated, expectations that cannot be met at the time because the design and development of reinforcing services in other program areas are not susceptible to fast development and reliable operation. Unfulfilled or blocked expectations can lead to a disillusioned rejection of the community program as a whole. Consequently, concerns of timing, emphasis, and balance become critical when organized neighborhood stimulation is employed.

The other program component seeks to inform people about available services and self-help opportunities. Means of communication are geared to the natural communications channels of the target areas. Neighborhood communicators who have the reputation for passing along reliable and authoritative information and who, because of their understanding of the special circumstances of families, know what specific information will be applicable in particular instances, are of critical importance. Indeed, even the understanding and use of information communicated through the general media of newspapers, radio, and television, so it appears, are strongly influenced by the interpretations of the members of the neighborhood who are recognized as authoritative communicators.

The general structure of the community action program is now modelled. The total program impact sought is socioeconomic change in the target groups. Presumably the nature and degree of change have been defined, and a time phasing of change projected. Three program areas have been selected for major strategic emphasis: education, employment, and social adjustment. Self-help action is generated by stimulating people to utilize services and to respond to opportunities. Within each program area are specifically defined program components, each a cluster of operating activities undertaken by a designed pattern of delegate agencies. Any delegate agency may be a multiple producer in that it may be operating several activities, each contributing to a different program component of a different program area. In this model, the activities of the various participating agencies are only the building blocks of the program as a whole. These component activities gain relevance and effectiveness only when drawn into the comprehensive system design of the total community program action system. The design, monitoring, and control of the action system become the critical determinates to total program effectiveness.

## Strategic Planning

It is central to this approach to program design to see the action process in its totality as a comprehensive system aimed at producing change in the community. The comprehensive system is a collectivity of operating subsystems producing activity components of the larger action complex. These subsystems must, so far as possible, complement each other. The nature, volume, and rate of their production, and its time-phasing, are integral to the total effectiveness of the comprehensive system. The design of the comprehensive system is a function of strategic planning; the guidance and balancing of the system in operation are functions of strategic control. The strategic system overlay is thus critical to general system effectiveness.

What considerations apply to selecting the producing subsystems, and incorporating them into the comprehensive system? The community context of the target area is likely to have certain developed and producing agencies, and certain others only partly developed but with useful potential. The complement of needed producers can be filled out with *ad hoc* undertakings, which may be needed particularly to provide means for the self-generated activities of the poor.

The first recourse should be to the developed and experienced agencies, for several reasons in addition to the obvious one of avoiding, if possible, the proliferation of operating agencies. Agencies in being and producing effectively have important potential for quick and knowledgeable response in a community-wide mobilization of productive capabilities. The established agency may have its inflexibilities, but these can probably be modified or compensated for with less time and effort than is required to develop and mature a wholly new agency. A further advantage to be sought is that of stimulating existing agencies to elaborate or to redirect their activities so as to deal more effectively with the poor. Their active participation in the community program may induce desirable change in these agencies. For example, an agency oriented to a lower income, middle class clientele may be stimulated to perceive and serve the special problems and needs of the poor. Of course, none of these potential advantages is guaranteed; all are contingent upon such variables as the characteristics of the agencies and constraints in the local environment. Each situation has to be evaluated realistically. There are other possible advantages which are also more problematical. The use of a battery of existing agencies as producers of services may give the strategic control function needed mobility and flexibility. It would eliminate or reduce commitment to maintaining an agency, which would be at least implied in the case of an *ad hoc* producer brought into being solely for the purposes of the community program. As to costs, the initial and developmental costs of a new agency are avoidable if an experienced agency is used. But this economy is also problematical. Obviously, a great deal depends upon the characteristics of available agencies. Their utility, that is to say potential effectiveness as intermediate component producers, can range from highly promising to negligible. Thus it is in order to consider the agency attributes that are likely to make significant differences, the dominant characteristics of organizations in the public, voluntary and private sectors.

*Public Sector.* In the public or governmental sector and such agencies as the local school system, the state employment service, and the public assistance system, the probabilities are that ongoing operations will be marked by relatively high energy, developed structure, and considerable operating momentum. A tendency to maintain ongoing patterns of operating behavior can be expected, and especially wherever highly programmed administrative action and structured, long-linked administrative technology are relied upon.

The question of the agency's formal authority to elaborate or adapt its operating objectives and patterns to the needs of the community program will arise in every instance. Beyond this is the question of the predisposition of the agency's social system to innovation, to response to fresh stimuli and changed orientation. Tendencies toward system closure, buffering against negative external feedback and accumulation of entrophic indicators, are warnings against heavy reliance upon participation. Probably participation is most likely to be effective where the agency has a demonstrated access to the target groups and an active interchange of feedback and response. In some instances a disposition to innovate will be present, inhibited only by constraints of funding and formal authorization which affiliation with the community action program can overcome. The best chances for effectiveness will be found where no basic changes in developed administrative behavior are involved, where the internal social system is predisposed toward the goals of the community program, the operating methods are functional, and the environmental supports are positive. Under these circumstances, the developed and stabilized productive capacity of the agency can be an important asset.

*Voluntary Sector.* In the voluntary sector, different factors are likely to be dominant. Continuing or permanent agencies are characteristically low energy systems as compared with those in the public sector. Often they are linked on the one side to a rather self-selected sponsorship in the community, and on the other to a limited and untypical clientele. They may or may not be professionally staffed and administered. In general they are more susceptible than public agencies to entrophic influences. But the input of fresh energy from the community action program can be a sound investment in some circumstances.

The chances for productive participation in the community program would appear to depend both upon the characteristics of the agency, and upon the type of service expected from it. Staffing characteristics are significant. A professionally oriented staff, alert and adaptive to changing needs in its field, and mobile in its capacity to relate to a poverty clientele, would be an important asset. The attitudes and expectations of the governing board and larger sponsoring group should be supportive of an expanded and redirected role for the agency. Material if less tangible characteristics are the agency's capacity to elaborate, to enlarge its field of activity, to add staff members from minority groups, and, in some cases, to move from an informal to a more regularized style of operation.

As to the type of service it can provide, the voluntary agency is likely to be engaged primarily in the use of a mediating or an intensive technology. Its emphasis is upon individualized problem solving, guidance, and counseling reinforcement. It should not be expected to change its method of operation, but rather to project its acquired competence to involvement with the poor. This may be difficult for an agency accustomed to serving a predominantly middle class clientele. The main advantage gained from involving the agency in the community program may be its reorientation to a poverty clientele, rather than the quality of its performance in the enlarged role. On balance, the use of the voluntary agency as a producer of services needs careful evaluation of the agency's potential in what will probably be a changed service role. The consequences of participation obviously can range from highly functional to completely dysfunctional.

*Private Sector.* The private sector is also a potential supplier of intermediate component producers. High energy, rather than low energy, systems can be expected here. The competitive survival of these organizations, by and large, turns upon their capacity to meet their operating and output requirements with an energy investment sufficiently less than the total of inputs that a prudent reserve can be stored to meet contingencies and to underwrite system elaboration. Consequently, their understandable tendency is to develop structured, programmed, and disciplined operating styles. System elaboration is likely to emphasize the extension of this style to additional areas of operating effort. In addition these organizations characteristically utilize a long-linked technology, in the production of tangible items, or an essentially mediating technology when sales and service activities are involved. Altogether, these administrative characteristics have limited applicability to problem solving needs of the poor. Probably the major contribution of private sector organizations is in job training and skill development. It goes without saying that this is not a simple undertaking. It is not limited to formal training. In most instances several social systems will be involved, among them the organized employees, the first-line supervisory groups, and the customer or client groups. In a way job training and skill development are only parts of a total undertaking to bring the disadvantaged person into the disciplined environment of employment and to reinforce his socialization in the special social system of the particular organization. There is an obvious, direct advantage where the trainees respond effectively and will be absorbed into the organization's work force. The further potential advantage is realized if changes in recruitment and employment practices are induced as a consequence of engaging in a purposeful, specially designed undertaking to develop members of the poor subcommunity into employable and productive persons.

*Ad Hoc Agencies.* The use of *ad hoc* agencies remains to be considered. This is another matter. The task of developing a new agency to produce problem-solving services is complex, especially in the social fields, unless it involves no more than replication of an effective agency with tested and transplantable methods, and operating in a similar environment. In any instance there is inevitably a period of operating design, staff socialization, and maturation. In the community program, the *ad hoc* agency is probably best adapted to the specialized functions of neighborhood organization, communication with the poverty groups, and possibly legitimation of the use of referral services to more specialized professional agencies. This observation is only speculation; much needs to be learned about the utilities, and the risks, of relying upon *ad hoc* agencies to supply elements of a comprehensive community program.

The foregoing sketch only suggests an approach to selecting intermediate component producers whose capabilities may be blended into a general system of community action. It is illustrative, not definitive. But the point is urged again that important considerations are involved.

## Unifying the Structure

Attention now turns to linking together the various producing units of the comprehensive community program into a coherent and balanced unity. This is the critical aspect of design. Implicit in the utilization of a variety of intermediate component producers, each with its own orientation and operating characteristics, is accentuation of the centrifugal tendencies observable in any complex program structure. A unifying network must be supplied. In conventional structures, reliance is usually upon a network of formal authority as an overlay upon the pattern of productive capabilities. This competence is used to establish a focus of central control from which delegations of operating authority are made, budgetary distributions are allocated, organization and operating methods authorized, progress is reviewed, and intervening corrective action taken. The system can function as a loosely decentralized confederation of essentially self-sufficient social systems; or, at the other extreme, it can be a tightly disciplined, closely integrated operating framework. But the comprehensive community program relies upon linkages of a quite different order. The unifying network is one of contract rather than of formal authority in the conventional sense.

An approach to the design of linkages can be presented only in broad outline here. It is necessarily tentative, because operating experience with program systems made up of diverse components is still to be analyzed and evaluated in depth. Initially it can be assumed that at least these factors are essential: contractual relationships designed to meet the unique requirements of the system; an information system that generates, feeds back, and interprets current experience; public liaison communication that develops general public, and especially clientele, understanding and reinforcement; and a program-wide strategic control system that can monitor ongoing developments and apply corrective or stimulating influences, within the contractual framework, as experience indicates. Each of these needs brief commentary.

*Contractual relationships.* This program design relies upon a network of contractual agreements to tie producing units into a coherent unity. The resulting relationships between general program control and the operating agencies, and among the operating agencies, cannot be expected to be as closely knit as in a tightly controlled formal organizational structure. The consequences for overall program effectiveness may range from functional to wholly dysfunctional, but the venture is a conscious and purposeful one. The positive utilities sought are using developed productive capabilities, minimizing the delays inherent in developing new operating units, involving all sectors of the community in a comprehensive effort, and inducing change in the orientations and objectives of the participating agencies. The risks are obvious. Agencies can be inflexible or reluctant to innovate, participating personnel can adapt poorly to changed roles, common goals shared by the agencies may never develop, and overall program strategy and control may fail. It would be folly to undertake the effort without a realistic understanding of the risks, and without a clear commitment to gain the potential advantages in spite of them. There should be no illusions, and thus no excuse for disillusionment.

The style of contractual agreement cannot rely upon stereotypes, if the system is unique. A sensible and obvious approach would be to build contract specifications around working relationships sought. At the outset there should be a clear expression of the objectives to be produced by the operating agency, and the activities to be employed in producing them. Pertinent here is the nature or identity of activities or services, rendered to what group or clientele, how identified as eligible, and under what pattern of priorities. Also important is the amount of activity, stated in performance units if possible, and the rate of activity also, if possible. The quality level is important but often difficult to specify. This consideration may be handled by defining the qualifications of personnel to be used, the nature of the performance unit, the outcome of individual case action, and the like. Then there are matters of the use of internal controls by the operating agency, such as supervision, monitoring, and reviews; the records to be maintained, both financial and operating; the reporting to be made to the point of general program control; and access to the agency and its records for audit and review both of financial transactions and of activity performance. What is involved here is the use of a disciplined, reliable method of operation, one that informs the agency whether it is living in accordance with its commitments, and what the outcomes of its efforts are. If the agency is well and realistically informed, full access to its information on the part of general program control should meet essential requirements. Some agencies, particularly those habituated to a very informal style of operation and *ad hoc* undertakings that inevitably must mature with experience, will find formally disciplined operation difficult and unwelcome. Some mutual accommodations may be inevitable. But systematized performance should be introduced from the outset. It is difficult to build up from a reliance upon informal, conventionalized behaviors which, while not necessarily dysfunctional in themselves, yield little information for overall analysis and evaluation.

There is also the question of payments under the contract. Probably most desirable is the pricing of output units, and payment on the basis of the number of units produced. When such units cannot be satisfactorily identified, pricing and payment may be based upon the number of activity units. The least desirable choice is payment on the basis of a working budget for the unit in being. In some instances, "seed" funding may be necessary. That is, an advance of working funds to develop and maintain the producing operation might cover anticipated costs for a limited period, three months for example. Then the working funds would be reimbursed for the units of output or activity actually produced. As a general rule, a reimbursement method of payment is preferable to underwriting an operating budget built up on the basis of objects of expenditure.

*Information System.* The need for a well-designed information system has been reiterated. The proportions of the system can be sketched, but the specifics of design will be specialized to fit individual situations. The following questions need to be asked as a beginning to design. What data are needed for the purposes of monitoring experience under the current operating program, of testing the effectiveness of program efforts, and of projecting future program plans? What are the sources of these data, and are special sensing devices needed to generate them? What processing and interpretation are needed to make them useful bases for decisionmaking? These questions should be answered with several program levels in mind. The operating unit will have its information needs for internal control. At the program component level there will be requirements to underpin that stage of analysis and interpretation. The synthesis of program component information into a program area analysis will follow, and finally analysis of the comprehensive program as a whole. Thus the information system will generate data required for interpretation at successive levels with, for the most part, the outcomes of analysis communicated to support interpretation on a broader scale at the next level. With these answers in hand, the system can be modelled by identifying information inputs by identity and source, programming processing and analysis to meet the requirements of the several levels of decision-making, and ordering outputs by sequence, content, and points of delivery.

*Public Liaison System.* The information system is intended to meet internal information requirements. There is the further need for public liaison, the transmission of information to external groups, and the generation of feedbacks from them. The purposes are to develop and maintain public understanding, to develop general public support and reinforcement, and to stimulate participation by clientele and potential clientele by informing them about available service opportunities, points of access, and channels for reporting experience. The considerations of information channels, media, and communication methods are pertinent. They will not be explored here; each community situation has its own needs and resources. The system has to be designed to fit the circumstances.

In summary, at this point, the comprehensive program can be seen as designed flows of purposive activity, reaching from the productive efforts of a collectivity of operating agencies producing components of major programs, through major programs interrelated in a comprehensive action effort aimed at producing change-inducing impacts in the community. Essential coherence, balance, and effectiveness rely upon the design of the contractual arrangements with the producing agencies, a comprehensive information system, a public liaison system, and strategic control. The idea of strategic control, its functions, and approaches to its design will be considered in the next chapter.

## Selected References

The action system approach is explained with reference to an operating agency in the paper George A. Shipman, "An Experimental Action Systems Model of Complex Governmental Organizations," Preston P. LeBreton (editor), *Comparative Administrative Theory*, University of Washington Press, Seattle, 1968, pp. 81–91. The modelling of an intervention system is explored in Fremont J. Lyden and George A. Shipman, "Activity Design," reproduced in Fremont J. Lyden, George A. Shipman, and Morton Kroll, *Policies, Organizations, and Decisions*, Appleton-Century-Crofts, New York, 1969. The ideas used in the present text are closely related to those employed in the papers cited.

For a basic understanding of the systems approach, valuable references are Karl Deutsch, *The Nerves of Government*, Free

# SIMPLIFIED MODEL OF A PROGRAM ACTION SYSTEM

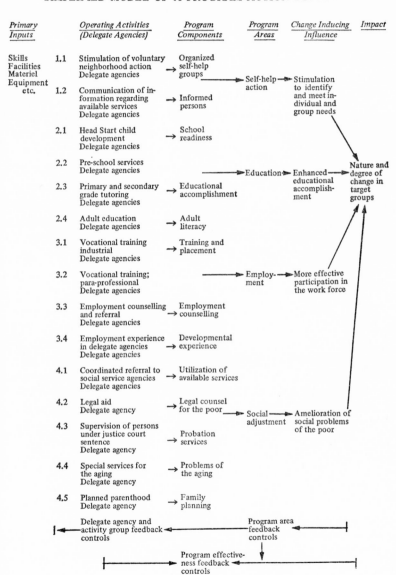

Press, New York, 1963; Stafford Beer, *Cybernetics and Management*, John Wiley and Sons (Science Editions), New York, 1964; Robert Boguslaw, *The New Utopians*, Prentice Hall, Englewood Cliffs, 1965; Daniel Katz, and Robert L. Kahn, *The Social Psychology of Organizations*, John Wiley and Sons, New York, 1966; and C. West Churchman, *The Systems Approach*, Delacorte, New York, 1968.

For an excellent discussion of technologies used by complex organizations, see James D. Thompson, *Organizations in Action*, McGraw-Hill, New York, 1967, pp. 15–19. This volume is a major contribution to the understanding of organizations.

Change in organizations as a consequence of participation in a community action program was analyzed by Fremont J. Lyden and reported in *Research Report No. 10* (Preliminary and Final), in *Final Report, Social Change Evaluation Project*, University of Washington, Seattle, 1968. The use of path analysis to attribute change influences is especially important.

# IV

# The System in Action

THE SYSTEM IN ACTION IS THE SUBJECT OF THIS chapter. For perspective, it may be useful to recall in summary the import of preceding chapters. The starting point was an attempt to analyze the problem of urban poverty; to define, in effect, the differences between conditions observed and conditions desired. A strategy of intervention was designed to abate these differences; that is, to alleviate the symptoms and to rectify the causes of poverty so far as either, or both, could be reached. The intervention strategy was translated into a program action system by factoring major action areas into their program components, and the components into operating activities. Agencies with appropriate capabilities were mobilized from the public, voluntary, and private sectors to produce the required activities. These agencies were joined in a systems relationship calculated to maximize the community resources toward a comprehensive attack upon poverty in the local context. The agencies, or activity producers, are linked by contract in this community action system, which, because of its special attributes, relies for coordination upon the network of contractual relationships, comprehensive information and public liaison systems, and a function of strategic control.

Strategic control is the guidance of system behavior toward realization of system objectives. From a theoretical standpoint, cybernetic ideas contribute to understanding the dynamics of this steering function. A particular insight from cybernetics is that of control as relying upon feedback readings to determine whether system operation is functioning as intended, and within acceptable tolerances. The readings may signal action to intensify the efforts that seem to be effective, to reexamine the apparently ineffective ones, to pull deviating activities back into the pattern of the action plan, or to stimulate the laggard. The capability for exercising the control function depends upon whether its essentials have been designed as components of the system, and whether operation of the system is effectively managed.

Strategic control is considered here in the special context of the comprehensive community action system, to gain a broad understanding of its function in the community action program. To that end, the essentials of the system are identified and its operation characterized. Many technical aspects are bypassed, not because they are unimportant, but because they become large and intricate concerns in themselves.

Strategic control functions in reliance upon four major resources: first, a projected program operating plan that forecasts the nature, rate, and cost of activity at critical points in the operating cycle; second, a carefully designed information system that senses, collates, and records data regarding the experience of the operating program; third, the analysis and interpretation of experience against the background of the operating plan and the observed effects of variable constraints and unforeseen contingencies; and, fourth, a battery of corrective measures that can minimize the developments appraised as dysfunctional and reinforce those found to be functional. Essential also, if implicit, in strategic control are the exercise of balanced, disciplined judgment and forbearance from ill-considered action prompted by anxiety.

## The Operating Plan

The program action system supplies the structural framework for expression of the strategy of intervention. The expression of the strategy in action has to be factored into an action plan for a determinate time period. A year is the usual period. It may or may not correspond with the calendar year, but an annual operating cycle is projected. Its essential elements are several. The objectives to be realized must be so defined and described in terms of identity, amount, rate, cost, and quality that clear-cut evaluations can be applied to outcomes. The required inputs of resources to sustain the expected operating level must be projected. Always important, but particularly difficult at the outset of a social change effort, is a target of the amount and kind of change the operating cycle is expected to produce. An operating projection should not be limited to a single annual cycle. At least three years should be used, with the next ensuing year rather tightly programmed and the years beyond it forecast in more general terms. As the program gains both experience and maturity, a five-year perspective is arrived at by adding the last completed year and the current year to the future three for a time span of operations inclusive of past experience, current developments, a short-term projection, and a longer-term forecast. Within this time frame objectives are set, experience evaluated, and accommodations introduced to respond to changes in fiscal support, in the environment and in the apparent effectiveness of effort.

The effect upon the operating plan of the rather special character of the comprehensive community program must be recognized at this point. In the usual program system, one that can be rather tightly linked and closely controlled, heavy reliance will be put upon feedback information to gauge the operation. It is often possible to employ a form of continuous search for program impact by using exploratory probes, developing and reinforcing activities showing external response and effectiveness, and dropping the less productive. This style of flexible program operation has many advantages. But it is not applicable in all situations. The alternative is a plan, developed usually by applied research methods, that undertakes to identify the relative degrees of priority in program effort, to time-phase activity, and to forecast outcomes. Fully developed, such a plan becomes an operating commitment. As a basis for delegation of operating responsibility, or for contractual agreements, the developed plan becomes nearly essential. But it can be inflexible, and can become dysfunctional if the planning analysis erred, or circumstances unexpectedly change. A program system linked by authority relations can use a combination of the plan and feedback approaches. A system that depends upon contractual linkages, as does the community action system, has less flexibility. Operating changes based upon feedback analysis would be limited to the scope of contractual commitments. This hazard, the loss of operating mobility because of contractual relations, will be considered again later.

*The Goal Structure.* The community system is also a special case in the matter of goal structure. A program action system having a variety of activity producers probably spanning the public, voluntary, and private sectors must expect a rather diffuse goal structure. Each established agency in participation is likely to have developed values and goals deeply rooted in its sense of special identity. For the purposes of producing elements or subcomponents of programs, a degree of goal diversity need not be dysfunctional, depending upon the nature of these goals and the ways they influence agency behavior. A substantial complementarity of separate agency goals is important. All, for example, need to put an overriding value on the problems and needs of the poor rather than upon the social or economic problems of the non-poor. If an additional objective is to induce change in agency goals through their participation in the comprehensive program, allowance must be made for goal dissidence. How much interim goal disparity can be tolerated with the expectation of ultimate goal complementarity is an open question.

*Projecting Operations.* The point has been made that the action plan, the projection for the operating cycle, expresses the strategy of intervention. To see its parts, and to understand how they interlock with the program action system, a sketch of its more important features may be useful. The practical approach to its formulation is to begin with the desired outputs, the change-inducing influences to be produced, and then to work back through the production process to arrive at the intermediate specifications. Unless reliable output-unit pricing has been established, and this would be unusual for social products of this nature, the method of working from desired outputs to inputs, pricing the results, reworking the mix and pricing again, may have to be repeated to arrive at a workable relationship between available resources and projected outputs.

The total comprehensive program output is the sum of the outputs of the several major programs. For the purposes of this illustration these programs are education, employment, social adjustment, and self-help action. Assumptions developed from the strategy of intervention and the identified characteristics of the poor are used to arrive at a distribution of effort among these program areas. Within each one, further decisions determine the mix of program components, as school readiness, educational accomplishment, and adult education in the example of education. The activity mix of each of the program components has then to be determined, and at this point the producing agencies should be identified. Thus a series of decision points are required. At each one the primary question is the optimal mix of action components that will produce the desired productivity at each stage of the program system. These are essentially strategic decisions; they amount to the distribution of resources so as to realize a high level of productivity and impact in relationship to the resources applied.

Additional considerations are also important. There will be questions of time-phasing. Newly initiated activities require "start-up" time before their productivity becomes available. When timing interdependencies exist among activities in the same or in different program areas, the mechanics of scheduling is important. For example, if a job-training effort is to be initiated, and its development is programmed for a particular segment of the operating cycle, the communication of information, the stimulation of interest, and the recruitment of trainees must be phased accordingly. Thus linkages and cross-feeding among the various component activities should be projected; this is the substance of coordinated action. In addition, the rate of productivity for each activity should be projected, with estimated levels of resource obligation and of output production set for monthly or quarterly readings, as the case may be.

The program projection should allow for variable constraints. The time and effort required to penetrate the poverty subcommunity with information about available services and to elicit participating response may be greater, or even less, than estimated. "Start-up" time for new activities may be longer than expected. The labor market may make placements difficult. Possibilities of this sort always exist; the operating plan should take them into consideration by building in flexibilities in timing and emphasis that can compensate for deviations. Of course, the rate of commitment of budgetary resources must be scheduled in balance with the projected rate of program activity. Relationships between budgetary obligation rates and program operating rates should be projected so that progress readings can be taken and interpreted.

Program analysis should also be projected and scheduled. What evaluations of experience should be made at what times? What analyses are needed to support these evaluations? What data and other information are required for these analyses? What are the sources of data and the processing requirements? The answers to these questions will underpin the design of reporting, processing, analysis, and interpretation of ongoing experience. This is a scheduling task in itself and one too often overlooked. The operation of strategic controls depends upon the reliable design and performance of the information system.

In a brief overview, these are the main elements of the operating plan. It is a disciplined framework within which scarce resources are to be committed with the expectation of measurable results. Ideally it is a careful balance of operating commitments, reserving flexibility to cope with deviations from projections and often wholly unexpected contingencies. This balance is likely to be difficult to realize in a comprehensive program built around contractual agreements. The built-in risks of the contract system are unavoidable, but with experience ways may be found to minimize them. The possibilities will be considered later.

*Strategic Control.* A well-developed, realistic operating plan is indispensable. So also is the information system. Essential information upon internal operating experience is generated through activity reporting. This reporting network itself has to be meticulously designed and faithfully maintained. Under any set of circumstances, strategic control sees the reality of experience through the perceptions of the reporting system. If reporting is incomplete, inaccurate, delayed, or skewed, reality is distorted and confused. The capacity for effective control is impaired.

The structure of the control system can be seen as an overlay upon the designs of the program action system and of the operating plan. The operating plan has projected the specifics of productivity for each of the activity producers; a sub-control function operates at the point of this production and feeds its results through the information system to the next point of control. The second point of control is concerned with program components. Here again the operating plan has established the expected readings for each stage of the operating cycle. These data are built up from the reports of the activity producers and, with the interpolation of other essential information, the framework for control is set. The process occurs again in a larger context for each of the major programs. For the comprehensive program as a whole the pattern of operating experience is synthesized, corrective action taken or proposed is reported, and the behavior of external variables, which will be explained, is interrelated. Thus the point of strategic control for the program as a whole is able to evaluate operating experience against the projections of expected developments and to determine what, if any, corrective intervention is needed and indeed possible.

In a comprehensive community program built upon contractual relationships, special problems are highly probable. Such experience as is available indicates that reporting requirements are difficult to enforce. Too often they were not designed in advance and built into the contractual arrangements; their administrative requirements and costs were not anticipated. In addition, many of the activity-producing agencies are not geared and disciplined to produce reliable reports. This has been the case with smaller, rather informal voluntary agencies and it is a major hazard with inexperienced *ad hoc* agencies.

Even with substantially accurate and complete reporting, interpretation is difficult because trends have not been established and experience is thin. Variations are hard to understand in the absence of the accumulated perspectives of an experienced operation. And further complications arise in the effort to identify and quantify external variables, such as the labor market, civic disorders, and the like, and relate their impact upon reported operating experience. These difficulties are likely to discourage efforts at developing and refining an effective information system and this tendency is a serious hazard in itself. Only through persistent and sustained effort can any information system reach the level of effectiveness that is needed for the operation of meaningful strategic control.

*Experience Analysis.* The analysis of experience necessarily works within a framework of working assumptions. Only in this way can interpretation be disciplined and reliable. One set of working assumptions has been referred to in the discussion of the operating plan. Specific activities have been projected to be produced at an assumed rate and at an assumed cost. The characteristics of these activities have also been assumed. To an extent, observable outcomes have been anticipated. These assumptions set baselines for the reading of reported experience. Some range of deviation from the projected rates is expected. As experience accumulates, working "pars" can be arrived at, and relatively normal deviations from these "pars" accepted as within a self-correcting range. Other influences are taken into consideration. One set of variable influences can be seen as internal. These operate within the framework of the operating programs; their effect can cause variations from expected experience beyond the normal range of deviation. For example, recruitment lags, slow equipment deliveries, and delays in availability of working space are familiar causes of low productivity. Other variables are external to the operating con-

text. Every program is conditioned by some pattern of constraints, most of which are variables. The significant point
here is that the intensity level is influenced by causation origi-
nating in the environment. Examples applicable to a community
program would be unforeseen changes in the employment level
which leave trained persons without job opportunities, or increased in-migration rates which change the composition of the
poverty groups. Still other external developments can be classed
as contingencies: events or influences not within the range of
reasonable expectations, a kind of latent risk such as a storm,
flood or fire of major proportions. Working assumptions would
in time allow for some degree of variations caused by internal
variables and by external variable constraints. Where the expected program experience is drastically upset by these variables, all projections become obsolete and new projections
become necessary. The occurrence of a major contingency also
requires rescheduling of productive activity. In other words,
some types of developments can be seen as normal variations
within a range of self-equilibrating influences, while others will
so disrupt the ongoing operating plan as to require complete re-
construction and redesign. Differentiating between routine and
traumatic development is at the core of strategic skill.

Each operating activity has its own critical points of observation, points for the sensing of significant trends and developments. Recurring points are input rates, such as the number of
cases or persons brought into the activity cycle, through-put
rates, the level of program activity at stages of case processing
and indications of the apparent quality level of effort, and output rates, the number of cases closed, trainees placed, and the
like. The rate of obligation of funds or the consumption of
other resources, and, whenever possible, data upon apparent
unit cost trends need to be related to the activity data. With
such information at hand, a realistic sense of trend and normal

variation can be accumulated over time. A caution here is against intervening prematurely or compulsively before a trend pattern is evident.

*Corrective Action.* The design of strategic control culminates in intervention; that is, in the introduction of changes in operations to reinforce constructive trends or to correct for dysfunctional trends. Where, as in comprehensive community action, the linkages connecting activity production and the exercise of controls are contractual, inflexibilities during the program cycle are unavoidable. These can impair the exercise of strategic direction. The design of the program can compensate for this risk only in part. For example, the contractual agreement can specify the nature, rate, quality, and unit cost of production by a participating agency. In addition the agency can be obligated to exercise internal controls to assure that its obligations are met. Then strategic control is primarily concerned with enforcing the agency's commitment to monitor its own operation in accordance with its agreement. But the utility of this arrangement is limited to situations where a change or redirection of the agency's original activity role is not indicated. Where a change is needed, different circumstances arise. Probably the most effective way of dealing with the possibility of change is to build options into the program plan. If the possibility of redirection of activity can be anticipated, and provided for in the contractual agreement as an option that can be exercised during the life of the contract, limited flexibility may be gained. Another possibility is the reservation of contract cancellation, but the use of this device has obvious difficulties. In all probability, many agencies would hesitate to enter into contractual agreements, gear themselves to required performance, and risk the possibility of cancellation through no fault of their own.

Following are the examples of the types of intervention that strategic control might exercise. Stating them does not mean that they are invariably available or applicable. They are only among the possible devices. Changes in the mix of activities may be possible. If agreements with producers permit, the amount of an activity may be increased in order to intensify effectiveness. If viable alternatives exist, producing agencies may be changed to replace a marginal producer with one more effective. The design of an activity may be changed. For example, short-term job training may be dropped in favor of training for a longer period or in a different skill. In some instances, the production of an activity may be accelerated or decelerated by revision of the contract. Deceleration is more difficult. Where unit costs are clearly out of line and not consistent with the contract, the producer may be forced to analyze his operations and take remedial action. Where output is not occurring, a review of reasons for lack of productivity may be undertaken.

As is commonplace in contract administration, the use of these intervention methods is not easy, particularly when both contracting parties are relatively inexperienced in this style of administration. This possibility that control may be nearly inoperable is one of the serious hazards of the contractual structure.

Strategic control is difficult to design and sensitive to exercise. Nevertheless it is an essential to the effective administration of the type of action program under discussion. Organizationally, the location of the control function is at the point of program administration, the program administrator for the comprehensive community undertaking. Again, it is important to notice that in this design the functions of program administration are planning, contracting, controlling, and evaluation, and do not extend to direct management of the actual production of component activities. Production is the responsibility of the several contractors.

*The System in Action: Evaluation*

Evaluation, as the exercise of measured, disciplined judgment, develops from the testing of effectiveness. The evaluation of any program effort has to be based upon a set of working criteria. These consist of the expectations of the results or outcomes projected in the operating plan. They are the outputs and impacts the plan is intended to produce as a consequence of the investment of designated resources applied within a context of known constraints.

All other characteristics of the plan also apply. The first questions are: Was the operating plan followed, and did it produce the outcomes projected in the plan? The second and more difficult set of questions is: Was the plan itself sound and effective? Were the outcomes, outputs, and impacts sound and effective influences in producing the results sought, the policy objectives embodied in the program? Would some other level of investment or distribution of emphasis among activities or program components have produced a greater impact? Should the operating plan be substantially replicated for ensuing operating cycles, or should a redesign be undertaken? Attempts to answer these questions encounter different degrees of difficulty. Approaches will be considered and then a general strategy of evaluation will be suggested. The possibilities for meaningful program evaluation depend primarily upon continuing program analysis.

*Testing Impact.* In testing the effectiveness of program action, a first choice would be to measure the change made through the program effort, assuming, of course, that the change embodies the policy objective. This approach encounters a number of difficulties. Where the policy objective is socioeconomic change, and where the change-inducing products of the program are mainly intangible social influences, it is hard to arrive at objective, quantifiable entities. In addition, and the case of urban poverty is a good example, meaningful measurement of total impact requires that the desired impact be reduced to a workable index of change. An experimental, working measure might be applied, but the possible range of error raises serious questions about its utility. Also there is the puzzling problem of isolating the effect of the program-generated change from that generated by wholly external influences, such as variations in the local economy, working in the same environment. Because of these difficulties, the inclination is to rely upon the measurement of change realized through specific component actions of intervention.

This second choice is a variety of suboptimizing. Its utility depends upon a number of factors. The controlling assumption is that certain attributes of poverty characterize the whole condition of poverty; and, if these attributes are reduced in incidence, poverty itself has been reduced. The reliability of such assumptions has already been explored; the hazards of error are substantial. But it is possible to project the impacts sought through various intervention efforts, such as preschool education and job training, and to assess the outcome of these efforts with respect to the persons reached by the various activities. An estimate of overall operating impact can be built up from a battery of these separate measurements, assuming, of course, that the desired change is identifiable and measurable over a relatively short time span.

While this second choice is clearly more operational than the first, its applicability depends upon the generation of data that measure activity output, and the differences in the clientele group attributable to the effort. The impacts of specific interventions are not readily isolated. Comparisons with control groups would add precision, but would also necessitate according services to some and denying them to others among potential clientele in comparable circumstances. It is obvious that unless program data are available to measure the nature and volume of program output and impact over some reasonable period of time, little yield can be expected of this effort.

A third approach is possible. This consists of some combination of exploratory probes and experimental activity styles. A set of probes can be applied at selected points of impact or transition to test the apparent effects of intervention. These can be designed to trace the consequences of involvement upon a selected sample of cases to determine the nature and degree of change taking place. The difficulties and hazards are obvious, but the intensive analysis of a sample of cases may yield more reliable insights than a more generalized estimate of impact upon the clientele as a whole. Also, it has the potential of yielding understanding of the interacting effect of multiple activities upon an individual or family group, and of building toward appraisal of the relative utility of one activity as compared with another.

These three approaches to the testing of program effectiveness undertake to identify program impacts and, so far as possible, to attribute various aspects of change to one or another of the specific component efforts. These are external tests; they are not aimed at the internal styles or operating methods of activities. To develop working evaluations of alternative operating modes in relation to apparent effectiveness, the experimental activity can be used. For example, differing designs of preschool education may be used for comparable groups of children, and the outcomes compared. Significant differences in outcomes may or may not be found. If they are, they can guide the redesign of the activity. The requirements for precise experimental design, data collection, and comparative analysis are self-evident.

*Operating Effectiveness.* The counterpart to external tests of program effectiveness is internal tests. These are concerned with the characteristics of the action process as distinct from the appraisal of external impact. The use of internal tests, of course, encounters the problem of associated variables. It becomes necessary to attribute a strong probability of effective action to an intervention process having selected critical characteristics. When these characteristics show change over a period of time in a way that would appear to enhance operating effectiveness, a strong presumption of greater program impact is regarded as possible.

The rationale is rooted in ideas about system reliability. Suffice it to say that simple operating efficiency should not be regarded as critical. Particularly in the case of a new undertaking, or one undergoing substantial change in orientation, considerable slippage is to be discounted. Until the systemic properties of the action flows have become stabilized, until subsystems have found their linkages, and until feedback controls are fully operative, appraisal is difficult. A process of maturation occurs. Until sufficient time has elapsed, tests are no more than preliminary and tentative.

The tests that appear to be most applicable, however, can be identified. Some may not be operational in a particular context; related ones may prove feasible. In any case, a few illustrations characterize the approach. A rather obvious case is the clientele orientation of the community agency, in which change is sought from lower-middle-income or middle-income groups to the poor. An agency may be brought into the comprehensive community program as an activity producer with the intent of influencing a change in its clientele orientation. If this change occurs, particularly in the direction of the hard-core poor, it may be assumed that participation in the community program has been a significant influence and especially so if the change stimuli can be traced to its community program linkage.

With respect to the operating characteristics of an agency, the central question is whether the action process has acquired increased reliability. It can be assumed that, as the action process matures, it will stabilize and that more standardized, more predictable measures will be used. This is a form of maturation in program behavior. Some indicators may be these: a movement toward professionalization of staff with increased value put upon professional training both preservice and inservice; the use of professionally disciplined methods of problem-solving and the reliance placed upon the use of professional conditioning in the application of intervention measures; the development of styles of decision-making that are relatively stable, well understood and predictable in use; the reliability of action processes in responding to identical or analogous situations; and the predictability of action responses to perceived stimuli. The reading of these indicators, particularly in the case of a relatively young operation, should yield insights into the extent to which the internal social system is developing as a coherent functioning entity.

A related set of observations applies to the level of social cohesion reached by the various operating systems, and to the relationships among them. The nature and the level of conflict among participants, individuals, and group in the action process is significant. This view requires discrimination between healthy competition and dysfunctional conflict. The former tends to stimulate effort without undermining the complementarity of perceived goals. The latter drains energy from expressive action and exhausts it in internal friction. The healthy system develops a capacity to contain potentially dysfunctional conflict and to resolve troublesome issues through disciplined

problem solving. Related are the behavior responses to perceptions of critical situations, pressing and threatening problems
to which developed behavior patterns seem inapplicable. What
situations are perceived as critical and how leadership, both
formal and natural, responds to them, are indicators of effectiveness. Compulsive, punitive, or panic responses reflect basic
social disorganization. The capacity to contain critical situations and to meet them with disciplined and, if need be, innova-
tive responses indicates basic strength.

In another dimension, it is important to develop a capacity
for using experience to increase perceived effectiveness. Living
by feedback requires substantial confidence and security on the
part of an administrative group. Reliance upon some self-
justifying dogma is easier. The alert and healthy activity provides for the generation of feedback information to inform it of
the consequences of its activities. Then arise the questions
of whether this information is used in an objective and systematic way, and whether responses are deliberate and controlled
rather than compulsive and punishment-oriented.

The foregoing observations lead to the question of the
capacity for innovation. An emotionally mature administrative
group should be able to identify opportunities for experimentation with new or at least different approaches. It is not threat-
ened by innovating change; it tests innovation objectively and
self-critically. When pressed to innovate by the needs of the
environment or by the development of new administrative
technology, it does not retreat into avoidance or go into
stereotypy.

Finally, there arises the question of the use of available
resources. A trend toward more disciplined and systematic use
of resources should be expected as experience accumulates.
If this occurs, observation should disclose internal controls,
perhaps quite informal, aimed at weighing the allocation of

resources to various efforts and objectives against apparent productivity. Thus ideas of marginal costs, opportunity cost, and cost-benefit ratios, however expressed, should be evident in the agency's evaluation of itself. If they are, what is the agency's capacity to reallocate the use of resources, shifting the emphasis of action so as to build upon apparently successful experience or to adjust to changed circumstances or fresh perceptions of needs? The absence of this capacity, the tendency to maintain any pattern once committed, would be indication of a tendency toward ineffectiveness.

In this connection, it is attractive to speculate upon the applicability of planning-programming-budgeting to a program structure based upon contractual relationships. An extended exploration of this question will not be attempted here. At various points in the preceding examination, ideas basic to program budgeting have been used. Certainly, prudent strategic program control would be continuously engaged in the appraisal of effectiveness even though, at an early stage of the approach, results of analysis lack desirable precision and concreteness. Nonetheless, it is possible to proceed on the basis of both experience and experiments to factor options in program design, and to test alternative mixes of component activities. More precise analysis will be contingent upon the development of better validated understanding of causal chains regarding the condition of poverty, and of the relationships between social impact in the community and the output of various change-inducing influences. Along with these, the capacity is needed to quantify both output and impact, to reduce both to unit costing, and thus to bring a much greater degree of confidence to the effort as a whole.

This chapter has been concerned with some of the salient characteristics of the program system in action, emphasizing the aspects that appear to have primary importance in guiding and controlling a comprehensive community effort of this special nature. Much of the commentary is unavoidably incomplete and open-ended. At this point in the development of the art and the discipline, sorely needed experience and technological development are still to come.

*Selected References*

Regarding cybernetic ideas, see Deutsch, *op.cit.*, Part II; Beer, *op.cit.*, Part II; Chadwick J. Haberstroh, "Control as an Organizational Process," reprinted in Walter Buckley (editor), *Modern Systems Research for the Behavioral Scientist*, Aldine, Chicago, 1968, pp. 445–448; and Leonard R. Sayles, "Accommodating for Change," reprinted in Lyden, Shipman, and Kroll, *op. cit.*, pp. 228–239. The idea of strategic control is really an application of cybernetic ideas.

For insightful commentaries upon the evaluation of broad-aim, broad-impact programs, see the articles by Weiss and Rein, and by Campbell, *op.cit.* The study by Lyden, *op.cit.*, is an excellent illustration of an approach to the testing of organization change.

# V

# Perspectives and Challenges

THE TIME HAS COME FOR AN OVERVIEW OF PER-
spectives, for recounting points of major significance and for a
sampling of the more apparent problems and challenges. It
should be emphasized again that this effort is far from a definitive analysis. The purpose is to stimulate reflection, not to express firm conclusions. Several items should be touched upon:
the nature of broad-aim, broad-impact programs, and the systems approach to modelling such efforts, the American Federal
System as a framework for program action systems, and the
role of the community. Beyond these are questions about the
state of the art and science of administration to come to grips
with projected trends.

*Broad-Aim, Broad-Impact Programs*

Programs such as poverty, model cities, and, indeed, protection of the environment are well characterized as "broad-aim"
efforts. The end sought is significant change in an existing state
of affairs, an elimination of conditions regarded as dysfunctional to societal values, and a redirection of long-term trends

deemed to be destructive. Efforts of this sort deal with deeply rooted patterns in the economy and the society; the problems are not so much new as they are intensified by an acceleration of their perceived consequences, and, so it would seem, more urgent because developing societal values make these consequences increasingly less tolerable. But a compelling desire to reverse trends and to produce other and more acceptable circumstances more agreeable to now dominant values cannot ignore the sunk costs, both economic and social, of the institutionalized ways of life that are concomitants, if not causes, of the conditions in which all basic change is sought.

In a sense, these broad-aim programs seek the replacement of one set of values, usually implicit rather than clearly affirmed, by another set susceptible to only generalized and often hortatory expression. Such an effort is difficult to operationalize, to translate into disciplined, controlled activities designed to produce clearly defined end results. Many problems are encountered. The basic causative factors, aside from set attitudes and ingrained behavior patterns, are not well understood. The observed, the objective characteristics of the condition to be dealt with are probably symptoms rather than basic causes. By and large, so far as is now known, there are no simple chains of causation. The observed attributes would appear to be a complex network of interrelated causes and effects but the nature of this relationship in any one context eludes the disciplined understanding essential to confident and reasonably predictable intervention.

Under these circumstances, intervening effort has to be exploratory and experimental. The risks are high. Specific outcomes cannot be guaranteed. The chances are spread among no effect, minimal effect, and dysfunctional effect. Because socioeconomic change is sought, any appreciable effect will be perceived as threats in some quarters. Activism on the part of the non-white poor, intensified competition in the labor market, larger investments in social services, and shifting complexes of political power can be expected to stimulate resistance to the program effort. And the resulting attacks will find any vulnerable target area that circumstances supply. Thus any broad-aim undertaking is likely to be caught between the premature expectations of some groups and the deep anxieties of others. But if the effort is to be undertaken at all, at the present state of knowledge, it has to proceed along a course of exploratory probes and experimental activities, persistently pursued but continuously tested for effectiveness, working toward a clearer understanding of the nature of the basic problem, and the utility, under one or another set of circumstances, of dealing with it effectively. Unavoidably this is a high-cost undertaking in terms of outcomes sought.

All the program products, including the intermediate or component elements, are intangible social products. They lack the concreteness and tangibility of physical improvements, for example. The more intangible the products, the wider the variation in perceptions of their nature and utility; and the wider the range of perceptions, the more diffuse the responses of the general citizenry. There is a strong temptation, under such conditions of uncertainty and ambiguity, to estimate that what is really sought is not so much a tangible, measurable outcome as a feeling that because of the investment of effort a difference somehow has been made. Thus there may be a lowering of the level of anxiety produced by the sense of major problems about which actually little of importance is being done. This condition indeed is not unique; there would appear to be elements of anxiety reduction in nearly every field of public effort. Public education and national defense are interesting examples. But in most fields of public activity there are tangible intermediate products, operating approaches are relatively institutionalized, and program momentum has been accumulated. Thus confidence, whether justified or not, has developed in the efficacy of familiar activities. Conventionalized approaches acquire tough roots and tend toward self-perpetuation. To be sure, perennially serious questions are raised and a ritual of reconsideration is celebrated. A measure of innovation may reassure the doubtful; the cycle continues. A new broad-aim effort lacks the roots of institutionalized activity. It is exposed to unique hazards and threats. In its maturity it will doubtless be identified by different names and symbols which erase the memory of the early stages of frustrating search and experimentation. The cutting edge of major socio-economic change is not an easy or comfortable location, and especially so if a diversity of expectation and a sense of critical urgency dominate the task environment.

*The Use of Systems Ideas*

Systems ideas can be used to build an experimental model of a broad-aim, broad-impact program undertaking. A model of this type does not attempt a definitive theoretical explanation of the nature of the problem or of the cause-effect chains characterizing it. The utilities are much more modest. A very preliminary and tentative construct is sought as a beginning point for placing key factors in a working relationship with each other so that the implications of various sets of assumptions can be seen and the bits and pieces of relatively hard knowledge can be put into a general framework. Such was the point of view of the first chapter.

At the outset, the field of interacting forces out of which the problem emerges can be seen as a natural system. A rough working model can be developed depicting the perceived problem. The assumed basic causes and the evidences of its incidence can be arrayed in assumed relationships. A complex of interacting and interdependent forces culminating in the production of societal dysfunctions results. It is to be expected that the precise nature of these forces is only dimly seen and understood, and that their interaction and the identification of the independent and dependent variables are not verified. Available knowledge can be applied to arrive at plausible assumptions. Also assumptions, however tentative, about the behavior of the system, its boundaries, and its cross-feedings with other systems can be interpolated. The points at which critically important verification is needed can be mapped. From this starting point, a strategy for clarifying the critical points of ambiguity can be projected. But whenever pressures for action are intense, there are only limited opportunities for systematic research. Experimental probes may be the only feasible possibility.

In the case of programs of this sort, there will usually be deep public concern over the experienced consequences of the problem, and a demand that effective intervention proceed. But the state of hard knowledge about causation and control may, and usually does, fall far short of support for confident intervention. Nevertheless action is urgent. Needs and pressures will not tolerate delay. Thus a calculated strategy of experiment and living by feedback may be the indicated path toward building a more refined, more reliable model of the natural system.

A working construct can be developed, identifying the assumed significant variables and the more potent causal paths connecting them. Then the assumptions for which hard, verified knowledge is needed can be identified and priorities can be set. Next an information feedback network can be built so that acquired data and insights, derived both from experimental probes and from generalized trends, can be sorted, channeled, and interpreted. Thus the elements of a strategy for search and clarification can be projected, aimed at an incrementally elaborated and tested construct of the natural system. This construct will never be fixed or static; it is developed and refined as experience accumulates to produce an increasingly useful understanding of the nature of the problem. This side of the systems approach, then, begins with a highly experimental construct of the natural system and projects a strategy calculated to bring it step-by-step closer to verified reliability.

The counterpart to the natural system model is a designed system construct. The designed system can be understood as an overlay of intervention action contrived to induce change in the behavior of the natural system, and if possible to redirect and control this behavior so as to avoid dysfunctional effects in the society. The construct of the natural system can be used to select the points of productive intervention, points at which apparent causal chains can be broken or possibly redirected, and dysfunctional outcomes modified. In the initial stages of the program the primary emphasis may be upon a massive undertaking to alleviate the dysfunctional consequences, but concurrently a battery of exploratory activities testing critical sets of assumptions can be geared into the total strategy of action. Feedback information would be generated to record the outcomes of those probes, and data analysis would be designed to interpret and record outcomes. As more reliable knowledge about basic causes accumulates, emphasis can gradually be shifted from allaying the symptoms of the problem to controlling the basic causes. Thus a strategy of healthy, rational incrementalism can be designed and applied toward accruing reliable understanding of the ways in which socio-economic values can be operationalized in the society.

This brief and greatly oversimplified sketch of a search and discover approach to problem solving in a broad-aim program leaves many aspects unexplained. The general emphasis is the perspective of the preceding chapters. The operating design has been merely sketched. Many of the obvious problems, hazards, and technical difficulties have been bypassed of necessity. Some of these will be commented upon later in this chapter.

## Federalism as an Action System

It is useful to apply this approach to the nature of contemporary federalism in the United States. With respect to major domestic concerns, the natural system can be viewed as encompassing the whole of the national economy and society. Indeed, in some instances, input and output interactions extra-national in scope will be identified. But for operational purposes, the problem to be dealt with—in its basic nature, causal paths, and impacts—can be viewed as nationwide in scope. Regional and localized variations can be seen as natural subsystems of the general system, with differing input and output mixes and identities. The designed system of intervention can also be modeled as a general system composed of a pattern of subsystems fitted to the special needs and characteristics of the natural subsystems.

The dominant patterns of action of the contemporary Federal structure can be interpreted in these terms. The fields of highway transportation, housing, social welfare, and, increasingly, education and outdoor recreation can be regarded as nationwide action systems with an interlocking among their unique interest groups, legislative components in Congress, the state legislatures and often local governing bodies, specialized public officials and employees, professional schools developing program specialists, a research program, and other shared resources. A structure of subsystems emerges with complex linkages and cross-feeding all designed to generate and channel the expression of social energy toward the realization of common expectations. Also, each level of the Federal pattern tends to be a subsystem with a specialized contribution to make to the vitality and effectiveness of the action system as a whole. The national level, for example, may supply the entrepreneural function and the generation of new technology, the states may serve as the distributors of the specialized resources and services, and the local units as producers of the program products. This, of course, is not an accurate explanation of any of the current program systems; it is only intended to make the point of the nature of a comprehensive action system.

If this point of view can be accepted as at least an experimental working model, present-day action processes aimed at meeting domestic needs can be understood as multi-jurisdictional, multi-sector in nature. Each component subsystem contributes some essential element. A fascinating question remains with respect to the general guidance and control function in each action system. The location is not immediately apparent and may not be institutionalized. It may operate in a quite unstructured, informal, even occasional way in response to needs and threats as these emerge.

### The Urban Area from the Systems Point of View.

The systems point of view can be carried through to the urban context. One interesting approach is to regard action in the community setting as predominantly a network of localized subsystems of nationwide action systems linked by local interdependencies into a discrete community-wide general system. This point of view needs a bit of commentary.

Community action—whether it is aimed at poverty, a model cities effort, urban redevelopment, economic development, or other concerns—has at least two dominant attributes. The first is comprehensive community effort. All available capacities and resources are mobilized to participate in the total undertaking. All sectors of the local society are enlisted, public, private, and voluntary, and in the public sector all agencies and jurisdictions are included. At least such is the aspiration. The second is the attribute of the community as the local subsystem manager. At this point the functions of subsystem design, operation, and evaluation are critical. The need may be met in a variety of ways. Organizational fragmentation often leaves a near vacuum of comprehensive concern and responsibility. By and large, the governing bodies were not developed, nor the members elected, to fill this type of role. Accrued civic expectations were narrower in scope and usually quite particularized. Structures of power and influence had similar dimensions.

Under the circumstances, the tendency in urban areas has been to respond to new problems by developing *ad hoc* problem-centered leadership groups. In some instances these have become anchored in the public sector. In others, the private or voluntary sectors have taken the lead, sometimes in one or another type of coalition. Usually these leadership groups have not been in a position to become producers of program products; they sought effectiveness as stimulators and coordinators of the agencies equipped with production capability. In the case of poverty, the tendency, contemplated indeed by the Federal legislation, has been to rely upon an *ad hoc* board upon which the urban area jurisdictions, the resource people, and the poor have been represented. An arrangement such as this can be no more than transitional. It lacks the tap roots of power, necessary for self-sufficiency and continuity. At the moment, however, few alternatives appear.

A further and quite fundamental question arises. It concerns the emerging role of the city as a governmental entity. Is the city to be just another producer of component program products, contributing according to its productive capability to some variety program action systems? Or is the city to be some-

thing more, to have a function closer to that of subsystem
manager and general urban system controller? At present, the
city government is often regarded as the fortress of change-
inhibiting forces. Can it turn itself about to become the catalyst
and manager of change?

In any case, the function of change strategist and subsystem
manager is indispensable. It will not remain empty. One interesting and challenging possibility is that the professional
administrative leadership of the new city will be the action
system manager, and the governing body the action catalyst.
Then the production by the city of public goods and services
would become a secondary concern, strategically less important than the city's role in subsystem development, guidance, and
evaluation.

## Challenges to Public Administration

The perspectives sketched in the preceding pages are essentially speculative. They are not firm predictions but rather
extrapolations into the future of the major trends examined
in the earlier chapters. The current emphasis upon broad-aim,
broad-impact governmental programs in the domestic sector
highlights them, although in many respects the main stream of
development in governmental action over the past thirty years
or so clearly shows these directions. There remains the question
of the impact of these developments upon the discipline of
public administration, and here the idea of discipline includes
the range of study, research, and professional practice. What
seem to be some of the salient influences upon the field growing
out of the trends that are now apparent? How do these influences point up the significance of various points of view, theoretical formulations, research strategies, and professional roles?
Several that now seem of major importance will be noted. Their

application is by no means limited to any particular field or sector of governmental action.

## Systems Approaches

The use of systems approaches in the social fields is relatively recent. Without attempting, at this point, to trace the origins of systems ideas, it may be said that these approaches have a special utility in the modeling and analysis of complex interactions of a behavioral and social nature. The idea of natural systems stems mainly from the biological sciences; it is especially useful for the experimental modeling of social phenomena where ongoing interactions among diverse sets of forces show persistent patterns and regularized outcomes. A problem field construct can be synthesized in this way, using available, more or less validated knowledge along with concepts underpinning the systems approach, to bring to awareness the assumed paths of causation and the extent to which assumptions are speculative.

The designed action system approach has developed mainly from the technological fields. It undertakes the disciplining of the design, operation, and evaluation of a coherent pattern of interdependent activities aimed at producing a set of desired results. In the social fields, this is a difficult undertaking. Systems are open, behavior is variable, and outcomes tend to be indeterminate. Nevertheless the approach offers a way for handling a larger set of variables than is possible when less complex analytical means are employed. The use of the natural system and the designed system in combination has fruitful possibilities. The natural system is the field of phenomena which produces the societal dysfunction; the designed system is the means for intervention aimed at inducing change in the behavior of the natural system toward more functional societal effects.

There is much to be done in developing and refining this type of systems approach to the point where it may become a primary means for the disciplining of public action. Its special strength is its focus upon the dynamics of action and interaction overriding the statics of forms and structures. The idea of the action process as the input, processing, and output of social energy has great potential for the deepening of analytical understanding.

In another and related way systems approaches seem on the way to important contributions. In the framework of these ideas, institutions become complex, value-based patterns of action and behavior rooted in the culture or often in specialized subcultures. Organizations can be understood as purposive social instruments, conditioned by natural system attributes derived from the special subcultures or social systems with which they interact, and by the accrued expectations and role requirements of the participants. In this perspective, the organization becomes a set of designed systems and subsystems overlaid upon and linked with the natural system attributes. The objective is to realize an effective processing of social energy toward the production of desired social products. This framework of ideas holds major promise in the development of a much more rigorous and more effective approach to the design and operation of purposive public action.

## The Structuring of Action

In structuring a course of action, the traditional, and in many quarters the preferred, method has been to view the program as a structure of authority. Coherence and reliability were sought by using a hierarchical pattern, concentrating formal authority at the apex with lines of delegation and sub-delegation distributing specific responsibility throughout the hierarchy and with lines of control unifying all activity back to the apex of author-ity. The reality of this approach fails under the tests of exper-ience and of research. But that is another story. The significant point is that a program design relying upon linkages of formal contract is a different and challenging way for building a pro-gram structure. To be sure, many organizations that are osten-sibly structures of authority actually behave as patterns of in-formal working agreements. Delegations are negotiated; so also are allocations of resources. Operating responsibility is accepted in consideration of the assurance of the supports deemed essential. All this occurs as conventionalized administra-tive behavior within the internal social system. But a structure of formal contractual relations is another matter.

The use of contractual relationships to obtain program com-ponents is neither new nor unique. Contracting out construc-tion, design, research, some specialized services and the like are familiar. Usually these arrangements are employed to aug-ment the capabilities of the agency, to take advantage of the established competence of the contractor, or to realize econo-mies of scale. In the case of broad-impact programs, however, a program structure of contractual linkages between pro-ducers of program components and the point of program management goes considerably beyond the conventional use of contract. This approach potentially has unique utilities, because it provides a means for crossing jurisdictional lines and sector boundaries to assemble as wide a range of productive capability as may be applicable under the circumstances. It can be the means for building action with a local focus by utilizing all applicable public, private, and voluntary capabilities. Then also, where a spin-off impact upon the participating agencies is desired, such as induced change in their orientations and goals, the multi-sector structure may have considerable ad-vantage. But again, the design, operation, and control of a structure of contract raise serious problems of responsibility, coordination, and mobility. This is an area for research and experimentation.

## The Focus of Public Administration

Implicit throughout this discussion has been the question of the focal concerns of the discipline of public administration. This point may gain clarity by applying a variation of the Parsonian idea of systems levels in organizations. Three levels are identified, the first a strategic or institutional level which is primarily concerned with linking the productive capability of the organization to the environment. Here would be concern with inputs of support, defense against attack, the relevance of purpose, and the means-ends relationships of the organization's activities to the external impact sought. The second, the managerial level, has the task of maintaining internal cohesion and balance. It employs the familiar methods of resources procurement, allocation, and control; of manpower recruitment and development; of information generation, storage, and referral; and the like. Its activity flows are almost entirely internal; they are only incidentally external. The third level, the technical, produces the variety of program products. Its name identifies its emphasis, the use of technology of one sort or another to produce component products in the external world.

The primary interest of this inquiry has been in a strategic level function—the design, guidance, and evaluation of a program intended to produce selected impacts upon the socio-economic environment. Over the years, this level has had relatively minor emphasis in the field of public administration. The primary point of interest has been the managerial level and the techniques employed there. To an extent, the technical level has been an object of research and analysis, but the tendency has been to assume that technical operations were the domain of other disciplines.

The strategic level of administration action needs much more intensive and imaginative attention than it has yet received. It is not extravagant to suggest that systems approaches have the potential for developing a disciplined treatment of the strategic function. The point of view of a program as instrumental action is pertinent. Thus general action theory becomes a resource for probing the nature of macroactivity and its impacts. Program analysis and evaluation can move into a new perspective as an integral element of the action process with the special task of providing the steering function.

### The Administrative Generalist

There has been, and indeed there still is, a tendency to identify the generalist as a management specialist who is knowledgeable and skilled in the use of such techniques as organization and methods analysis, budgeting, personnel management, supply management, and the like. In the proximate future, the generalist will probably be a person with special competence in the design, operation, and evaluation of program action systems. He will be the professional specialist at the strategic level, the "systems manager." The managerial level will have its own specialist corps. A tendency in this direction seems evident. The specifications of the role are gradually taking shape. It seems reasonable to assume that the role requirements will extend beyond the scope of any existing academic discipline, and indeed beyond the experience acquired at either the technical or managerial levels. Altogether, a major weakness in American administration may be the lack of well developed, effective systems managers. Here is another challenge to the administrative profession.

*Selected References*

For fundamental perspective upon the nature of organizations, see the contributions of Talcott Parsons, *Structure and Process in Modern Societies*, Free Press, New York, 1961, ch. 1, 2; and "Components and Types of Formal Organization," LeBreton, *op.cit.*, pp. 3–19.

# Appendix

# Ideas from General Systems and Administrative Theory

SEVERAL IDEAS USED HERE ARE DERIVED FROM general systems theory or from general administrative theory. Since varying shades of meaning are associated with them in the literature of the administrative field, the meanings intended for them in these pages are explained below.

*General systems theory* can be characterized as dealing with the interaction of a set of components, continuing through time, where this interaction has some purpose or function of value to the system as a whole. For example, individuals relate themselves in groups for mutual reinforcement toward some common purposes. Such a group becomes a small, or micro-system. A number of these groups showing continuing interactions can become a larger system, and so on until the dimensions of a large or macro-system are reached. The micro-systems are then subsystems of the macro-system. This is an illustration of a *sociocultural*, rather than a *physical*, system because the components are social entities, human roles, behavior styles, shared expectations, and the like. The system is *natural* in the sense that it is not purposively designed and consciously controlled. It is a pattern of often spontaneous interactions. A *designed* or *rational* system, as the term suggests, is one put together for the purpose of realizing desired outcomes, and controlled toward that end. A complex organization is a useful example of a designed system, one that is usually an overlay upon, and shows linkages with, some pattern of natural systems expressing such social products as professional identities, operating behaviors, status stratifications, and the like.

Each system is assumed to have a set of characteristics necessary for the fulfillment of its purposes. There are inputs of energy needed to maintain the operation of the system, and of information and stimuli to guide operating behavior. A throughput process uses these inputs to support the system and to produce its products. Outputs are these products; they often become inputs for other related systems. *Feedback* is the return flow of information that tells whether the system is operating as expected, and enables adjustments to be made to preserve the reliability of the system's operation.

A system operates on energy from current inputs or stored from preceding surplus inputs. *Physical energy* is derived from physical sources; for example, the generation of electricity. *Social energy* is derived, as the term indicates, from social sources. The skills, competences, and enthusiasms of participants generate social energy. The throughput process requires some level of energy, from all sources, to maintain its vitality. It consumes some proportion of this energy, and expresses some in its output. If energy inputs are not sufficient to support the system, it tends to decay and ultimately to disintegrate. This tendency is identified by the term *entropy*. The idea of *homeostasis* is the tendency of the system to maintain its own equilibrium analagous to that of the living organism. *Equifinality* points to the working principle that several courses of action can lead to substantially the same outcome.

A further distinction is used, that of high and low energy systems. Systems operating at a high energy level consume relatively large amounts of energy, and their products have a high energy level. Such a system can be expected to generate a strong impact upon its environment. The low energy system is the opposite of the high. It is likely to be sluggish in performance, and to express only a minimum impact.

A classification of administrative technologies follows James D. Thompson (*Organizations in Action*, McGraw-Hill, 1967). *Long-linked technology* relies upon the interdependence of a series of steps, ordered serially so as to produce an end product. The production line is a familiar example. *Mediating technology* involves the linking of parties having complementary needs so that these needs are satisfied, such as the postal service, or any of the variety of governmental banking and insurance programs. *Intensive technology* is the undertaking of change-inducing or therapeutic treatment of particular clients, where each case is particularized and individually dealt with. These characterizations are oversimplified but the distinctions between the technologies should be apparent. Thompson also uses the idea of *task environment*, which denotes the total field and scope of interaction in program activity. Thus all parts of the society that participate in supplying inputs, imposing constraints, using outputs, and appraising effectiveness are components of the task environment.

*Suboptimizing* identifies an approach to estimating program measurement. It is often used where program impacts are so intangible or so long delayed in evidencing themselves that systematic observation of outcomes is not possible. Also program outputs, in turn, may be so difficult of identification that they can only be inferred from the nature, amount, and quality of efforts to produce them. Under circumstances such as these, precise measurement and more exact evaluation often are not possible. The alternative is to rely upon assumed cause-effect relationships. If presumably appropriate measures are taken (as intermediate steps in the program process), the effectiveness of the end result can be projected. The application of evaluation measures to these intermediate steps would be suboptimizing.

# Index

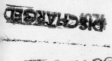